in search of understanding

THE CASE FOR CONSTRUCTIVIST CLASSROOMS

WITH A NEW
INTRODUCTION BY
THE AUTHORS

JACQUELINE GRENNON BROOKS
MARTIN G. BROOKS

Upper Saddle River, New Jersey
Columbus, Ohio

This special edition published by Merrill Education/Prentice Hall, Inc. by arrangement with the Association for Supervision and Curriculum Development.

Vice President and Publisher: Jeffery W. Johnston
Executive Editor: Kevin M. Davis
Editorial Assistant: Amy Hamer
Director of Marketing: Kevin Flanagan
Marketing Manager: Amy June
Marketing Coordinator: Barbara Koontz

The book was printed and bound by RR Donnelley. The cover was printed by RR Donnelley.

Jacqueine Grennon Brooks is Associate Professor in the Center for Science, Mathematics and Technology Education at the State University of New York at Stony Brook. E-mail: jgbrooks@notes.cc.sunysb.edu.

Martin G. Brooks is Superintendent of the Valley Stream Central High School District in Valley Stream, New York. E-mail: vsdist1@li.net.

31   16

ISBN: 0-13-060662-6

In Search of Understanding: The Case for Constructivist Classrooms

Dedication

For our parents and their grandchildren.

Acknowledgments

We consider ourselves fortunate to have worked over the years with groups of outstanding educators and students throughout the nation—most particularly in the Shoreham-Wading River (N.Y.) school district, the Valley Stream Union Free School District #13 (N.Y.), the Valley Stream Central High School District (N.Y.), and at the State University of New York at Stony Brook—who have permitted us access to their classrooms and their thoughts. Our interactions with and observations of these people have shaped our thinking. It is their work that we highlight in this book.

Introduction

Judging from our conference presentations, our consulting work, and our mail since the 1993 publication of this book, the basic tenets of constructivism clearly strike a responsive chord with a great many teachers and administrators.

Constructivism is a topic on the conference programs of virtually all prominent national educational organizations and has been widely described and analyzed in professional journals. Recent publications have presented constructivist theory in a variety of contexts: curriculum mapping, teacher education, and school leadership, to name three. University faculty and national teacher associations have endorsed constructivist lesson design and instructional practices. Moreover, a few state education departments (New York, California, and Kentucky, among others) have identified constructivist teaching practices as preferred, and have included explicit examples of student-designed work in their state curriculum frameworks and standards.

Learning: Not a Linear Process

Interestingly, all of these events have occurred at a time when the politics of education has taken a turn away from the principles on which constructivist-based education rests. The thinking behind this turn is exquisitely simple: develop high standards to which all students will be held; align curriculum to these standards; construct assessments to measure whether all students are meeting the standards; reward schools whose students meet the standards and punish schools whose students don't.

This simple, linear approach to educational renewal is badly flawed. It is virtually identical to all the other approaches to renewal that have preceded it, and it misses the point. Meaningful change is not accomplished through political pressure but, rather, through attention to the idiosyncratic, often paradoxical nature of learning. As many states are discovering, "raising the bar" by commandment results in a jump in high school dropouts, increased spending on student remediation and staff preparation for new assessments, constriction of curriculums as they are aligned with the new assessments, and loss of public confidence in schools as large numbers of students fail to meet the standards. Missing from this mix is evidence of increased student learning.

Why? Learning is a complex process that defies the linear precepts of measurement and accountability. What students "know" consists of internally constructed understandings of how their worlds function. New information either transforms their old beliefs or . . . doesn't. The quality of the learning environment is not merely a function of where the students "end up" at testing time or how many students "end up" there. The dynamic nature of learning makes it difficult to capture on assessment instruments that limit the boundaries of knowledge and expression.

Please note that we are not saying that classroom practices designed to challenge students in transforming their current thinking and student success on tests are inherently contradictory. However, there is much evidence (from NAEP [National Assessment of Educational Progress] and TIMSS [Third International Mathematics and Science Study], to name but two sources) that classroom practices specifically designed to prepare students for tests do not foster deep learning that is applied to new settings. This evidence has led many school districts to question the philosophical underpinnings of the long dominant pretest-teach-posttest model of education. Despite completing all their assignments and passing all their tests, too many students simply are not learning.

A Process of Making Personal Meaning

Consequently, many programs and curriculums recently adopted in districts throughout the nation and created not by political pressure but by teacher conviction and demand are centered around the notion that, classroom instruction notwithstanding, students make their own meaning. Examples of such programs include process writing, problem-based mathematics, investigative science, and experiential social studies.

In a constructivist classroom, the teacher searches for students' understandings of concepts, and then structures opportunities for students to refine or revise these understandings by posing contradictions, presenting new information, asking questions, encouraging research, and/or engaging students in inquiries designed to challenge current concepts.

In this book, you will read about the following five overarching principles evident in constructivist classrooms.

• *Teachers seek and value their students' points of view.* Teachers who consistently present the same material to all students simultaneously may not consider students' individual perspectives on the material to be important, may even view them as interfering with the pace and direction of the lesson. In constructivist classrooms, however, students' perspectives are teachers' cues for ensuing lessons.

• *Classroom activities challenge students' suppositions.* All students, irrespective of age, enter their classrooms with life experiences that have led them to presume certain truths about how their worlds work. Meaningful classroom experiences either support or contravene students' suppositions by either validating or transforming these truths.

• *Teachers pose problems of emerging relevance.* Relevance, meaning, and interest are not automatically embedded within subject areas or topics. Relevance emerges from the learner. Constructivist teachers, acknowledging the central role of the learner, structure classroom experiences that foster the creation of personal meaning.

• *Teachers build lessons around primary concepts and "big" ideas.* Too much curriculum is presented in small, disconnected parts and never woven into whole cloth by the learner. Students memorize the material needed to pass tests. But many students, even those with passing scores, are unable to apply the small parts in other contexts or demonstrate understandings of how the parts relate to their wholes. Constructivist teachers often offer academic problems that challenge students to grapple first with the big ideas and to discern for themselves, with mediation from the teacher, the parts that require more investigation.

- *Teachers assess student learning in the context of daily teaching.* Constructivist teachers don't view assessment of student learning as separate and distinct from the classroom's normal activities but, rather, embed assessment directly into these recurrent activities.

The Search for Understanding

The power of these five principles is compelling, but only to those not wedded to linear approaches to educational renewal. We acknowledge that, for some, it is easier to disseminate information from the front of the room, assign chapters from textbooks, and grade workbook sheets and exams than it is to help each student search for personal understanding and assess the efficacy of that search. And, it probably seems more reasonable to structure lessons around one right answer to each question than it is to value different, often contrasting, points of view. And, yes, it is presumably more comforting to think of all students as blank slates with similar cognitive profiles than it is to view them as individuals whose life experiences have shaped singular sets of cognitive needs.

Nonetheless, more and more teachers continue to gravitate toward constructivist principles because . . . well, because they make sense. Teaching and learning are complicated, labyrinthine processes filled with dead ends, false positives, contradictions, multiple truths, and a great deal of confusion. Trying to simplify and quantify the teaching/learning dynamic wrings out its essence and renders it a *reductio ad absurdum*.

Over the past several years, then, the case for constructivist classrooms has been strengthened and also has become more acute. Virtually all school districts profess to want their students to be thinkers and problem solvers. In the classroom, the individual search for understanding lies at the heart of this pursuit. The languid instructional practices of the past, even dressed in new clothing, cannot trick students into learning. Engagement in meaningful work, initiated and mediated by skillful teachers, is the only high road to real thinking and learning.

During a workshop several years ago, a teacher, reflecting on her own education, noted that the teachers who influenced her most were the few who made difficult concepts accessible by seeking to understand what she knew at the time. We have heard many people recount similar stories about their most memorable teachers. For the most part, these remarkable teachers mattered so much because they were less concerned about covering material than they were about helping students connect their current ideas with new ones. These teachers recognized that learning is a uniquely idiosyncratic endeavor controlled not by them but by their students, and they knew that conceptual understanding mattered more than test scores. These teachers are constructivists, and they're the ones we remember.

PART I
The Call for Constructivism

Honoring the Learning Process

Considering the Possibilities

Coming To Know One's World

1

Honoring the Learning Process

From the White House to the statehouse to the schoolhouse, politicians and educators have been wringing their hands over the condition of education in our nation. Some excoriate our present educational system, citing reports that raise questions about the inability of American students to perform as well on content area tests as students from other nations. Others are troubled by the condition of education in our nation for very different reasons. For a growing number of educators, questions regarding understanding and meaning and the roles that schools play in encouraging or stifling the search for understanding are far more important than questions regarding achievement as measured by test scores.

Many promising proposals have been put forth to address the issues surrounding students' construction of meaning. These proposals suggest overhauling assessment practices to make them more relevant for students, establishing site-based management teams in schools, rethinking the efficacy of tracking and ability grouping, and freeing school districts from federal and state mandates. We applaud these efforts, but find that these proposals don't quite go deep enough. They don't speak openly enough about the education system's underlying suppositions about what it means to learn, about what it means to become educated. They don't reach the nucleus of education: the processes of teaching and learning that occur daily, relentlessly, inexorably in classrooms throughout the nation. Educational reform must start with *how* students learn and *how* teachers teach, not with legislated outcomes. After all, the construction of understanding is the core element in a highly complex process underpinned by what appears to be a simple proposition.

The Construction of Understanding

It sounds like a simple proposition: we construct our own understandings of the world in which we live. We search for tools to help us understand our experiences. To do so is human nature. Our experiences lead us to conclude that some people are generous and other people are cheap of spirit, that representational government either works or doesn't, that fire burns us if we get too close, that rubber balls usually bounce, that most people enjoy compliments, and that cubes have six sides. These are some of the hundreds of thousands of understandings, some more complex than others, that we construct through reflection upon our interactions with objects and ideas.

Each of us makes sense of our world by synthesizing new experiences into what we have previously come to understand. Often, we encounter an object, an idea, a relationship, or a phenomenon that doesn't quite make sense to us. When confronted with such initially discrepant data or perceptions, we either interpret what we see to conform to our present set of rules for explaining and ordering our world, or we generate a new set of rules that better accounts for what we perceive to be occurring. Either way, our perceptions and rules are constantly engaged in a grand dance that shapes our understandings.

Consider, for example, a young girl whose only experiences with water have been in a bathtub and a swimming pool. She experiences water as calm, moving only in response to the movements she makes. Now think of this same child's first encounter with an ocean beach. She experiences the waves swelling and crashing onto the shore, whitecaps appearing then suddenly vanishing, and the ocean itself rolling and pitching in a regular rhythm. When some of the water seeps into her mouth, the taste is entirely different from her prior experiences with the taste of water. She is confronted with a different experience of water, one that does not conform to her prior understanding. She must either actively construct a different understanding of water to accommodate her new experiences or ignore the new information and retain her original understanding. This, according to Piaget and Inhelder (1971), occurs because knowledge comes neither from the subject nor the object, but from the unity of the two. In this instance, the interactions of the child with the water, and the child's reflections on those interactions, will in all likelihood lead to structural changes in the way she thinks about water. Fosnot (in press) states it this way: "Learning is not discovering more, but interpreting through a different scheme or structure."

As human beings, we experience various aspects of the world, such as the beach, at different periods of development, and are thus able to construct more complex understandings. The young child in this example now knows that the taste of seawater is unpleasant. As she grows, she might understand that it tastes salty. As a teenager, she might understand the chemical concept of salinity. At some point in her development, she might examine how salt solutions conduct electricity or how the power of the tides can be harnessed as a source of usable energy. Each of these understandings will result from increased complexity in her thinking. Each new construction will depend upon her cognitive abilities to accommodate discrepant data and perceptions and her fund of experiences at the time.

Student Learning in Schools

Accepting the proposition that we learn by constructing new understandings of relationships and phenomena in our world makes accepting the present structure of schooling difficult. Educators must invite students to experience the world's richness, empower them to ask their own questions and seek their own answers, and challenge them to understand the world's complexities. Duckworth (1993) describes her version of teaching thusly: "I propose situations for people to think about and I watch what they do. They tell me what *they* make of it rather than my telling them *what* to make of it." This approach values the students' points of view and attempts to encourage students in the directions they have charted for themselves. Schools infrequently operate in such a way, as they typically narrow the band of issues for students—and teachers—to study, demand short and simple answers to questions, and present complexity as previously categorized historical eras, mathematical algorithms, scientific formulas, or pre-established genres and classes.

But schooling doesn't have to be this way. Schools can better reflect the complexities and possibilities of the world. They can be structured in ways that honor and facilitate the construction of knowledge. And they can become settings in which teachers invite students to search for understanding, appreciate uncertainty, and inquire responsibly. They can become constructivist schools. Noddings (1990) writes:

> Having accepted the basic constructivist premise, there is no point in looking for foundations or using the language of absolute truth. The constructivist position is really post-epistemological, and that is why it can be so powerful in inducing new methods of research and teaching. It recognizes the power of the environment to press for adaptation, the temporality of knowledge, and the existence of multiple selves behaving in consonance with the rules of various subcultures (p. 12).

Starting with What We Know

To effectively explore our educational system, we must first examine the core unit of the whole enterprise, the classroom, a setting we already know much about. First, the American classroom is dominated by teacher talk (Flanders 1973, Goodlad 1984). Teachers often disseminate knowledge and generally expect students to identify and replicate the fields of knowledge disseminated. In a flowchart of classroom communication, most of the arrows point to or away from the teacher. Student-initiated questions and student-to-student interactions are atypical.

Second, most teachers rely heavily on textbooks (Ben-Peretz 1990). Often, the information teachers disseminate to students is directly aligned with the information offered by textbooks, providing students with only one view of complex issues, one set of truths. For example, many teachers validate the textbook view of Christopher Columbus as an intrepid explorer in search of a new world. The revisionist view of Columbus' voyage as the cause of oppression of the Native-American population in North America is not frequently discussed in classrooms. Alternative interpretations of social phenomena are rarely considered.

Third, although there exists a growing interest in cooperative learning in America's schools, most classrooms structurally discourage cooperation and require students to work in relative isolation on tasks that require low-level skills, rather than higher-order reasoning. Think about, for example, the many elementary classrooms in which students sit alone for portions of almost every day completing workbook and ditto sheets.

Fourth, student thinking is devalued in most classrooms. When asking students questions, most teachers seek not to enable students to think through intricate issues, but to discover whether students know the "right" answers. Consequently, students quickly learn not to raise their hands in response to a teacher's question unless they are confident they already know the sought-after response. Doing otherwise places them at some risk.

Fifth, schooling is premised on the notion that there exists a fixed world that the learner must come to know. The construction of new knowledge is not as highly valued as the ability to demonstrate mastery of conventionally accepted understandings.

Perceived Success

The power and sanctity of the curriculum and the subordination of students' own emerging concepts are profound concerns. Many students struggle to understand concepts in isolation, to learn parts without seeing wholes, to make connections where they see only disparity, and to accept as reality what their perceptions question. For a good many students, success in school has very little to do with true understanding, and much to do with coverage of the curriculum. In many schools, the curriculum is held as absolute, and teachers are reticent to tamper with it even when students are clearly not understanding important concepts. Rather than adapting the curriculum to students' needs, the predominant institutional response is to view those who have difficulty understanding the unaltered curriculum as slow or disabled. These students are often removed from mainstream classes, given remedial instruction, or retained.

Even students who are capable of demonstrating success, who pass tests with high marks and obtain "honors" diplomas, frequently don't connect the information they receive in school to interpretations of the world around them. Consider Gardner's (1991b) lament:

> I contend that even when school appears to be successful, even when it elicits the performance for which it has apparently been designed, it typically fails to achieve its most important missions. Evidence for this startling claim comes from a by-now overwhelming body of educational research that has been assembled over the last decades. These investigations document that even students who have been well-trained and who exhibit all the overt signs of success—faithful attendance at good schools, high grades and high test scores, accolades from their teachers—typically do not display an adequate understanding of the material and concepts with which they have been working (p. 3).

In many districts throughout the nation, students spend a good deal of time preparing for standardized tests or statewide exams. For example, in mathematics, a geometry teacher might help students memorize the formulas and proofs necessary to pass an exit or minimum competency exam. A few months later, however, when some of these same students are asked to apply geometric principles on a national examination, such as the National Assessment of Educational Progress (NAEP), only a small percentage of them might demonstrate the ability to do so (Schoenfeld 1988). In other words, although considered successful in a high school geometry course, many of these students cannot demonstrate facility with geometric principles, even when their learning was assessed in the same manner as it was previously assessed, specifically, on a multiple-choice exam.

Katz (1985) and Gardner (1991b) describe the discrepancy between perceived and actual success as the difference between learning and performance. In discussing this difference, Katz (1985) stresses that emphasis on performance usually results in little recall of concepts over time, while emphasis on learning generates long-term understanding. Students educated in a setting that stresses performance learn that technique, rules, and memory matter more than context, authenticity, and wholeness. Therefore, rather than seeking deep understanding, these students seek short-term strategies for accomplishing tasks or passing tests. When asked, several weeks or months later, to apply what they supposedly had learned, most students can't.

Making a Difference

The debate that frames current conceptions of school reform was largely defined decades ago. Franklin Bobbitt (1924, p. 8) wrote: "Education is primarily for adult life, not for child life. Its fundamental responsibility is to prepare for the 50 years of adulthood, not for the 20 years of childhood and youth." The current critiques of American education emanating from business and industry certainly have their roots in Bobbitt's conception of the purpose of schooling. John Dewey (1938), however, argued that education as preparation for adult life denied the inherent ebullience and curiosity children brought with them to school, and removed the focus from students' present interests and abilities to some more abstract notion of what they might wish to do in future years. Dewey urged that education be viewed as "a process of living and not a preparation for future living."

Schools and the teachers within them can do both: they can be student-centered and successfully prepare students for their adult years by understanding and honoring the dynamics of learning; by recognizing that, for students, schooling must be a time of curiosity, exploration, and inquiry, and memorizing information must be subordinated to learning how to find information to solve real problems. Adult modeling and environmental conditions play a significant role in the development of students' dispositions to be self-initiating problem posers and problem solvers. When students work with adults who continue to view themselves as learners, who ask questions with which they themselves still grapple, who are willing and able to alter both content and practice in the pursuit of meaning, and who treat students and their endeavors as works in progress, not finished products, students are more likely to demonstrate these characteristics themselves. Barzun (1992) writes:

> Anyone who has ever taught knows that the art of teaching depends upon the teacher's instantaneous and intuitive vision of the pupil's mind as it gropes and fumbles to grasp a new idea (p. 20).

Similarly, when the classroom environment in which students spend so much of their day is organized so that student-to-student interaction is encouraged, cooperation is valued, assignments and materials are interdisciplinary, and students' freedom to chase their own ideas is abundant, students are more likely to take risks and approach assignments with a willingness to accept challenges to their current understandings. Such teacher role models and environmental conditions honor students as emerging thinkers.

Considering Developmental Principles

Students' cognitive developmental abilities are another major factor in the process of constructing understanding. It is crucial that teachers have some understanding of the foundational principles of cognitive developmental theory. For example, in one kindergarten class, children watched their teacher mold three buckets of clay into eight balls each and give one ball to each child. Most of the students "correctly" counted the twenty-four balls and acknowledged that each child got a "fair" share. Did the students actually *know* that when the teacher divided the clay each ball became 1/8 of a bucket and 1/24 of the total amount of clay? They were in the room and they saw it happen. But, the children in this kindergarten class were intellectually busy grappling with other relationships and understandings. They were engaged in notions of counting, distributing, and matching, important undertakings in the development of their concepts of number. Most of them didn't consider the ball of clay 1/8 of one total and simultaneously 1/24 of another total. They did not construct the concept that fractions imply relativity. They *did* construct and consolidate many other concepts. They seriated numbers and established a one-to-one correspondence between students in the class and balls of clay, constructions meaningful to them.

To maximize the likelihood that students will engage in the construction of meaning, teachers must interpret student responses in developmental terms and must appreciate those terms. For example, in discussing how children come to understand number, Papert (1988) writes:

> Children don't conceive number, they make it. And they don't make it all at once or out of nothing. There is a long process of building intellectual structures that change and interact and combine (p. 4).

Teachers who value the child's present conceptions, rather than measure how far away they are from other conceptions, help students construct individual understandings important to them.

The Simple Proposition Revisited

The proposition that we construct individual understandings of our world and the assertion that schools must play an important role in this process does sound simple. But what sounds simple propositionally is quite difficult operationally. Consider this example of a first-year middle school teacher preparing for opening day in a school noted for its constructivist orientation. Her journal entries describe her lesson planning process:

9/2
Here it is, Labor Day, the day before I start my new job. I'm scared to death. Last week, I had a meeting with my team teacher. We talked about what we are going to teach for the first few weeks. It was very sketchy. She also talked about something called "the big picture." I'm not quite sure what she meant. She gave me an example. If only I could remember it now. We're starting the microscope unit. Oh, that's another thing. I always thought that we would just follow the textbook. She tells me to "start thinking in terms of units." If I could only get an opening to start this unit off with, I'd be a little more at ease.

11

9/3

... Tomorrow with the kids I have to have a grabber lesson. Tomorrow, I'm THE TEACHER. My team teacher told me to get an idea of what the microscope unit is all about. Nothing has come to me yet. Perhaps, if I could only relax, I could think.

9/4

It happened! This morning around 4 a.m. I got an idea. A microscope "takes a closer look at life." My topic today was "Taking a Closer Look at Life." I paralleled a story about people wanting to take a closer look at what was happening at the scene of a fire to taking a closer look through a microscope lens. Not a very close analogy, but, in a sense, it worked. ...

The teacher opened her first lesson with the question: What do you think life science is all about? A few students responded with one-word answers such as "living," "animals," "plants." She acknowledged each student with "Yes" or "That's right." She then read a story about a fire engine. Immediately upon finishing the story, she said to the students: "The point of the story is that you can see many things at a fire and you can see many things in science. Everyone come to the front and get your textbooks." After some administrative work took place, the teacher handed out photocopies of some well-known optical illusions and said: "In science, you have to develop a critical eye. Write down what you think you see." Her next questions were: "Who can see a vase?" and "Who can see two faces?"

The teacher's lesson plan had many of the elements of a constructivist approach, but her implementation of the plan did not. She opened the lesson with an umbrella question that asked students to share their current points of view. But she accepted one-word answers, asked for neither elaboration on the part of the speaker nor feedback from the group. She planned for an analogical discussion with students. But, she, herself, drew the analogy *for* the students rather than asking questions that would have allowed the students to generate their own analogies. She attempted to integrate her "science" topic with literature and art, encouraging the students to challenge their own perspectives. But *she* defined the range of perspectives by asking if the students saw a vase or two faces before the students had time to determine for themselves what they were seeing.

The new teacher took delight in her generation of the "Taking a Closer Look" theme and designed a carefully structured plan to share her creativity. But, in doing so, she limited the students' opportunities to tap into *their* creativity. The lesson was not an invitation to explore the theme. It was a methodical telling of the theme.

This example suggests that becoming a constructivist teacher is not simple. It requires continual analysis of both curriculum planning and instructional methodologies during the process of learning to be a teacher, reflective practices for which most teachers have not been prepared.

Most teachers agree with the quests and goals of the constructivist orientation: teachers want students to take responsibility for their own learning, to be autonomous thinkers, to develop integrated understandings of concepts, and to pose—and seek to answer—important questions. Some teachers, though, have difficulty practicing constructivist methodologies. The pathway to becoming a constructivist teacher meanders through our own memories of school as students, our professional education, our deeply held beliefs, our most cherished values, and our private versions of truth and visions for the future. Bruner (1986) writes:

> "[W]orld making" . . . starting as it does from a prior world that we take as given, is constrained by the nature of the world version with which we begin the remaking. It is not a relativistic picnic. . . . In the end, it is the transaction of meaning by human beings, human beings armed with reason and buttressed by the faith that sense can be made and remade, that makes human culture and by culture, I do not mean surface consensus (p. 159).

It's important that we, together, explore the constructivist proposition and ways to put this proposition into practice.

References

Barzun, J. (1992). *Begin Here: The Forgotten Conditions of Teaching and Learning*. Chicago: The University of Chicago Press.

Ben-Peretz, M. (1990). The Teacher-Curriculum Encounter: Freeing Teachers from the Tyranny of Texts. New York: State University of New York Press.

Bobbitt, F. (1924). *How To Make a Curriculum*. Houghton-Mifflin, Boston.

Bruner, J. (1971). *The Relevance of Education*. N.Y.: Norton.

Dewey, J. (1938). *Experience and Education*. New York: Macmillan.

Duckworth, E. (April 30, 1993). Personal communication, presentation at Institute for Educational Dialogue on Long Island.

Flanders, M. (1973). "Basic Teaching Skills Derived from a Model of Speaking and Listening." *Journal of Teacher Education* 24, (Spring 73): 24-37.

Fosnot, C.T. (in press). "Rethinking Science Education: A Defense of Piagetian Constructivism." *Journal for Research in Science Education*.

Gardner, H. (1991b). *The Unschooled Mind: How Children Think and How Schools Should Teach*. New York: Basic Books.

Goodlad, J. (1984). *A Place Called School*. New York: McGraw-Hill.

Katz, L.G. (1985). "Dispositions in Early Childhood Education." *ERIC/EECE Bulletin* 18, 2. Urbana, Ill.: ERIC Clearinghouse or Elementary and Early Childhood Education.

Noddings, H. (1990). "Constructivism in Mathematics Education." *Journal for Research in Mathematics Education #4*. Reston, Va.: NCTM.

Papert, S. (1988). "The Conservation of Piaget: The Computer as Grist to the Constructivist Mill." In *Constructivism in the Computer Age*, edited by G. Forman and P.B. Pufall. Hillsdale, N.J.: Lawrence Erlbaum Associates.

Piaget, J., and B. Inhelder. (1971). *Psychology of the Child*. New York: Basic Books.

Schoenfeld, A. (1988). "When Good Teaching Leads to Bad Results: The Disasters of 'Well Taught' Mathematics Courses." *Educational Psychologist* 23, 2: 145-166.

2

Considering the Possibilities

Contrasting Paradigms

Constructivism stands in contrast to the more deeply rooted ways of teaching that have long typified American classrooms. Traditionally, learning has been thought to be a "mimetic" activity, a process that involves students repeating, or miming, newly presented information (Jackson 1986) in reports or on quizzes and tests. Constructivist teaching practices, on the other hand, help learners to internalize and reshape, or transform, new information. Transformation occurs through the creation of new understandings (Jackson 1986, Gardner 1991b) that result from the emergence of new cognitive structures. Teachers and parents can invite transformations, but can neither mandate nor prevent them. For example, after gazing at a block of wood for the first three months of his life, an infant who touches the block with his newly acquired grasping skill transforms his cognitive structures, and thus affects his understandings of the block. Virtually all infants do this. On the other hand, many high school students read Hamlet, but not all of them transform their prior notions of power, relationships, or greed. Deep understanding occurs when the presence of new information prompts the emergence or enhancement of cognitive structures that enable us to rethink our prior ideas.

Why doesn't more thinking and re-thinking occur in schools? Our position is that the mimetic approach to education is too compelling for many educators to give up. It is amenable to easily performed and widely accepted measurement, management, and accountability procedures. This approach has long dominated educational thinking, and, therefore, policymaking. If students can be trained to repeat specific procedures and chunks of information, then they are viewed as "having learned." The predominant ways in which students are asked to express this learning is through multiple-choice or short-answer tests. The typical manner in which teachers document this learning is through posting grades.

The constructivist vista, however, is far more panoramic and, therefore, elusive. Deep understanding, not imitative behavior, is the goal. But, capturing another person's understanding is, if anything, a paradoxical enterprise. Unlike the repetition of prescribed behaviors, the act of transforming ideas into broader, more comprehensive images escapes concise description. We see neither the transformed concept nor the process of construction that preceded its transformation. The only discernible aspect is, once again, the student's behavior, but a different type of behavior. In the constructivist approach, we look not for what students can repeat, but for what they can generate, demonstrate, and exhibit.

Traditional instruction often leads students to believe they are not interested in particular subject areas, such as physics or foreign language or literature. The constructivist paradigm holds disinterest less as a function of the particular subject areas than as a function of the ways in which students have been taught. Figure 2.1 summarizes some visible differences between traditional and constructivist learning environments.

Take, for example, two 7th grade science lessons on photosynthesis. In Mr. Randall's classroom, middle school science is taught through a combination of textbook work and teacher demonstration. Students perform experiments from time to time, depending upon the availability of materials and space. Students read a widely used 7th grade science textbook (Heimler, Daniel, and Lockard 1984), which explains that:

> Photosynthesis (foht oh sinh thuh sus) is the chemical change that produces food. In photosynthesis, carbon dioxide gas and water are combined to produce sugar and oxygen. The sugar may be changed to starch. Sunlight is necessary for photosynthesis. It supplies the energy for the chemical change. The energy becomes locked in the sugar and starch molecules that are produced (pp. 176).

FIGURE 2.1

A Look at School Environments

Traditional Classrooms	Constructivist Classrooms
Curriculum is presented part to whole, with emphasis on basic skills.	Curriculum is presented whole to part with emphasis on big concepts.
Strict adherence to fixed curriculum is highly valued.	Pursuit of student questions is highly valued.
Curricular activities rely heavily on textbooks and workbooks.	Curricular activities rely heavily on primary sources of data and manipulative materials.
Students are viewed as "blank slates" onto which information is etched by the teacher.	Students are viewed as thinkers with emerging theories about the world.
Teachers generally behave in a didactic manner, disseminating information to students.	Teachers generally behave in an interactive manner, mediating the environment for students.
Teachers seek the correct answer to validate student learning.	Teachers seek the students' points of view in order to understand students' present conceptions for use in subsequent lessons.
Assessment of student learning is viewed as separate from teaching and occurs almost entirely through testing.	Assessment of student learning is interwoven with teaching and occurs through teacher observations of students at work and through student exhibitions and portfolios.
Students primarily work alone.	Students primarily work in groups.

17

Mr. Randall then talks about the role of chlorophyll and presents the chemical equation for photosynthesis: $6CO_2 + 6H_2O \rightarrow C_6H_{12}O_6 + 6O_2$. The written explanation of the chemical equation indicates that when carbon dioxide and water are in the presence of energy (sunlight, in the case of photosynthesis), sugar and oxygen are produced. The sugar is used by the plant to make the cellulose that forms its cell walls and to make food for self-repairs and storage for later nourishment. Mr. Randall also describes the process of respiration, then reviews the information through a test at the end of the chapter that includes several question formats:

- True or False: "Food is produced in leaves."

- Circle one: "(Carbon dioxide, Sugar, Water) is produced in photosynthesis."

- Fill in the Blank: "Photosynthesis occurs inside plant cells that contain _____ ."

- Short answer: "How is respiration different from photosynthesis?" (pp. 183-185)

This is the mimetic approach to learning. Students commit new information to their short-term memory for the purpose of mimicking an understanding of photosynthesis on an end-of-chapter test. There is little in the presentation of the information or the assessment strategies that challenges students' current beliefs about the way plants grow and the relationships among plants and other life forms. In fact, both the way in which the content is presented and the manner in which learning is assessed militate against the development of such understandings, and instead encourage rote memorization of a symbolic, chemical equation.

Contrast this approach to a second classroom, one in which the teacher, Ms. Martina, not only deleted the molecular equation and references to cell walls in her introductory lesson plan, but actually deleted all references to photosynthesis. Ms. Martina asked her students to think of systems with which they might have some experience and familiarity, and to indicate the product created, the energy source needed, and the raw materials used. She asked her students to consider, for example, their art classes and what they create there. Several students taking a "home technologies" class at the time were making malted milkshakes. They combined ingredients (malt, milk, and cocoa) in the presence of an external energy source (an electric blender) to produce a product (the milkshake). They did not readily come up with a by-product. But when they lit on an "appetite-wetting aroma" as a possibility, they became quite animated. Another student, thinking of his health education class, described exercise as a system consisting of ingredients (a human body, weights, and exercise machines) acted on by an energy source (one's muscles) to generate a product (increased strength and muscle tone) and a by-product (a sense of well-being). These analogies generated enthusiasm about the students' home technologies and health class activities. The students engaged in interdisciplinary discussions with each other and Ms. Martina.

Ms. Martina structured her initial lessons on photosynthesis so that her students might consider and consolidate the aspects of a system. The term *photosynthesis* was not mentioned during the lesson. Barzun (1992) writes:

> It is not the subject but the imagination of [the] teacher and [the] taught that has to be alive before the interest can be felt (p. 63).

Ms. Martina asked her students to think of photosynthesis as a system in which certain ingredients (carbon dioxide and water) are changed by an outside energy source (sunlight) to produce a product (sugar) and a by-product (oxygen). The concept of a by-product, in and of itself, had been a new idea for most students and was an important precursor to understanding the "system."

It was important to Ms. Martina that her students consider the relationships among plants and other life forms and the role that photosynthesis plays in those relationships. The depth to which she might eventually pursue the chemical explanation of the topic depends on the strength of the framework the students construct as a result of the opening lessons.

Though Ms. Martina's students didn't construct a biochemical understanding of photosynthesis, and their examples were not completely analogous to the system of photosynthesis in terms of reversibility and complexity, they did begin to appreciate that one way of trying to understand photosynthesis is as a systemic process yielding both a product and a by-product. This understanding can serve as a basis for the construction of a more sophisticated understanding of photosynthesis and the ability to use the unit's vocabulary. Forman and Kuschner (1977), in discussing Piaget's ideas on the construction of knowledge, write:

> Think of the child not understanding some system, such as the game of baseball, to understanding that system. Knowing the entire list of rules would not be credited as knowledge, to Piaget. Knowing how to navigate the rules, to infer why it makes sense to hit the ball lightly, to figure out why the rules allow you to run past first base but not second—these examples of a generative use of the rules give evidence that the list has been constructed into a whole system (p. 84).

Ms. Martina's analogic activity served as an invitation for students to look at photosynthesis as a whole system. The students' own creation of analogies helped them to construct a framework. In order to complete the task, students asked questions about photosynthesis, no mean feat with 7th graders, and struggled to put the "answers" into a meaningful context.

Let's consider students' conceptions of photosynthesis in a teacher preparation class of graduates and undergraduates with biology and earth science majors. In one class, the professor asked the students to explain the process of photosynthesis in "simple," everyday terms. The following two responses demonstrate the tentative nature of their understandings: "It has something to do with making carbon dioxide." "No. it's not. The plant uses carbon dioxide to make . . . to make . . . a food molecule . . . I think?"

These are two college students enrolled in both a biology course and a teacher preparation course. They acknowledged embarrassment at not being able to describe photosynthesis concisely. In fact, they volunteered to reconsider the topic and give the class a mini-lesson at the next class meeting. On that occasion, they accurately, and enthusiastically, described photosynthesis on the biochemical level. They used sketches and models of the light and dark stage reactions and the Calvin cycle and described in detail the many molecular activities that take place during photosynthesis.

During the students' description of how chlorophyll gives off electrons, another class member asked, "Does the chlorophyll ever run out of electrons?"

After a contemplative pause, one of the presenters replied, "No, it has lots of them."

These two students offered the class a technically accurate description of photosynthesis. They demonstrated that they had the ability to memorize and recall information, and that they could effectively articulate this information to others. But they did not direct questions back to the information they had memorized. In other words, they had prepared their presentation as if they were about to take a fact-based, multiple-choice test.

Let's look at an excerpt from the journal of another student in the same methods class:

> Unfortunately, one of the lasting impressions I will have from this class was the series of disappointing responses I heard to your questions about photosynthesis. Clearly, most students in the class, aside from not remembering the details of photosynthesis (to some degree forgivable), were apparently not taught or made to appreciate its significance to life on this planet, energy flow through the food chain, atmospheric composition, and the elegant efficiency with which solar radiation is utilized by chlorophyll. I don't think you intended to make photosynthesis the topic by which you demonstrated the deficiencies of our educational system. However, that's how it turned out. The people in our class are reasonably intelligent. The limited understanding of a basic concept like photosynthesis, demonstrated this week, can only be the result of inadequate teaching. And, I suppose, it is this that we've been considering all along. (Ferrandino 1991)

Choosing the Constructivist Paradigm

When teachers recognize and honor the human impulse to construct new understandings, unlimited possibilities are created for students. Educational settings that encourage the active construction of meaning have several characteristics:

• They free students from the dreariness of fact-driven curriculums and allow them to focus on large ideas.

• They place in students' hands the exhilarating power to follow trails of interest, to make connections, to reformulate ideas, and to reach unique conclusions.

• They share with students the important message that the world is a complex place in which multiple perspectives exist and truth is often a matter of interpretation.

• They acknowledge that learning, and the process of assessing learning, are, at best, elusive and messy endeavors that are not easily managed.

To understand constructivism, educators must focus attention on the learner. But, opportunities for learners to learn are heavily controlled by the structure of schools. This book, therefore, often chronicles examples of teaching/learning interactions from the point of view of the teacher and the setting for the purpose of illustrating how the "people in charge" might begin to restructure the learning opportunities they make available in their settings. But we must *always* remember that in order to realize the possibilities for learning that a constructivist pedagogy offers, schools need to take a closer, more respectful look at their learners.

References

Barzun, J. (1992). *Begin Here: The Forgotten Conditions of Teaching and Learning*. Chicago: The University of Chicago Press.

Ferrandino, F. (1991). Unpublished manuscript. New York: SUNY at Stony Brook.

Forman, G., and D. Kuschner. (1977). *The Child's Construction of Knowledge*. Belmont, Calif.: Wadworth Co.

Gardner, H. (1991b). *The Unschooled Mind: How Children Think and How Schools Should Teach*. New York: Basic Books.

Heimler, C., L. Daniel, and J.D. Lockard. (1984). *Focus on Life Science*. Columbus, Ohio: Charles E. Merrill Publishing Co.

Jackson, P.W. (1986). *The Practice of Teaching*. New York: Teachers College Press.

3

Coming To Know One's World

onstructivism, as a way of coming to know one's world, is supported by a long and honorable body of literature and research, much of which is listed in this book's bibliography. We highlight here the works of a few philosophers, researchers, and theorists who have informed our thinking and practice and whose work underpins the constructivist teaching principles and descriptors we discuss in Parts II and III. There is clearly a connection between constructivism as an epistemological and philosophical image and constructivism as an educational framework.

Although some argue that the first great documented constructivist was Socrates, our discussion doesn't stretch that far back. In the more recent past, several philosophers, psychologists, and educators have struggled to understand the individual's relationship with nature and society and have helped us reformulate many of the fundamental questions we have asked ourselves. The nature of knowledge, and therefore of learning, has emerged over time as an essential line of inquiry.

The philosopher Emmanuel Kant, whose work bridged the 18th and 19th centuries, attempted to wed two disparate views of knowledge: the view that logical analysis of actions and objects leads to the growth of knowledge and the view that one's individual experiences generate new knowledge. Kant contended that both views have merit: analysis, by definition, occurs after the fact; sensate experiences occur before or during the event. Both are a function of one's own idiosyncratic mental filtering system. Kant concluded that one cannot infer new relationships among objects, events, or actions unless one has a priori views through which perceptions can be organized. These views affect how one makes sense of new information. Bruner (1986, p. 96) referred to these prior understandings as "mental constructions projected onto an 'objective world.'"

What Is Real?

One cannot have an interest in the notions of constructivism without grappling with questions of perception and reality. Is there one, fixed, objective world that we all struggle to come to know, or are there many different worlds, dependent for their definition upon individual perception? The psychologist George Kelly (1955) wrote of the relationship between perception and objective reality:

> Man looks at this world through transparent patterns or templets, which he creates and then attempts to fit over the realities of which the world is composed. The fit is not always very good. Yet, without such patterns the world appears to be such an undifferentiated homogeneity that man is unable to make any sense out of it. Even a poor fit is more helpful to him than nothing at all (pp. 9-10).

We concur. We once watched a seven-year-old child at the beach for the first time. When she first stepped off of the board-walk, she exclaimed with great surprise and discomfort, "The sand sticks between my toes!" We brushed the sand away and she happily took another step, then disappointedly said, "It keeps on happening." She made many other discoveries that day, a good number of which did not "fit" with her prior experiences.

Idiosyncratic constructions of prior experiences form the basis of the paradigms, the frameworks of thinking, we each use to perceive and consider the phenomena around us. Kuhn (1962), in his classic work, *The Structure of Scientific Revolutions*, uses the term "paradigm" to describe the lens that orders, but also limits, our perception and thinking. He uses the term "paradigm shift" to refer to the process that occurs within the individual who is able and willing to change his lens. Changing the lens is an internal process initiated by the individual when current rules and theories about the way one's world works no longer account for the information being perceived or provide for the job to be done.

For many educators, becoming a constructivist teacher requires a paradigm shift. Becoming such a teacher means much more than appending new practices to already full repertoires. For many, it requires the willing abandonment of familiar perspectives and practices and the adoption of new ones.

The Influence of Piaget

Kuhn's paradigm shift is similar to the description of accommodation offered by the well-known Swiss scholar, Jean Piaget, one of the most influential proponents of constructivism. Piaget was, by his own definition, a genetic epistemologist concerned primarily with cognitive development and the formation of knowledge. His research led him to conclude that the growth of knowledge is the result of individual constructions made by the learner. Piaget (1971) wrote late in his career:

> The current state of knowledge is a moment in history, changing just as rapidly as knowledge in the past has changed, and, in many instances, more rapidly. Scientific thought, then, is not momentary; it is not a static instance; it is a process. More specifically, it is a process of continual construction and reorganization (pp. 1-2).

Although Piaget's career spanned over 50 years and generated an extraordinarily substantive body of research, his work has gained varying levels of acceptance in American education circles. There are many reasons for this, not the least of which is Piaget's own reluctance to apply his notions to education. Another reason lies in the strong roots of American behavioral psychology in our educational system, exemplified by the work of Skinner (1938) and Thorndike (1926). These theorists and researchers described human behavior essentially by the stimulus-response relationship coupled with positive reinforcement of desired behaviors and negative reinforcement of unwanted behaviors. Other views of human behavior have been largely ignored in American education. Wadsworth (1971) writes:

> Traditionally, American psychologists of the behaviorist school do not infer the existence of internal mental processes (of thought). Piaget's concepts, like assimilation, are entirely foreign to the behaviorist position (p. 6).

Piaget viewed constructivism as a way of explaining how people come to know about their world. He buttressed this explanation with extensive documentation of behaviors he witnessed and with well-supported inferences about the functions of the mind. Piaget (1952) viewed the human mind as a dynamic set of cognitive structures that help us make sense of what we perceive. These structures grow in intellectual complexity as we mature and as we interact with the world we come to know and as we gain experience. Through maturation and experience, the groundwork for new structures is laid. For example, the cognitive structures required to comprehend that a wooden cube is hard are rudimentary and far less complex than the structures necessary to understand that a cube has length, width, and height, and that these three factors combine to determine the cube's volume.

An infant, yet unable to hold or manipulate the cube, defines it by the sides visible to her at that point in time. When the child's musculature and mental structures allow her to touch it, she is presented with new information that must be integrated into her thinking. An important cognitive structure has changed; the initial "nongrasping" structure has been refashioned into a new "grasping" one. This process is called accommodation. The child's newly created structure allows assimilation of the experience to occur within her mind.

In Piagetian terms, the temporary cognitive stability resulting from the balance of assimilation and accommodation is called equilibrium. Piaget suggested that the creation of new cognitive structures springs from the child's need to reach equilibrium when confronted with internally constructed contradictions; that is, when perception and "reality" conflict. The quest for cognitive equilibrium is among the most controversial of Piaget's notions.

Bruner (1964) and Chomsky (1977) have suggested that factors such as language and prior experience are more closely associated with the development of new structures than is the quest for cognitive equilibrium. A number of other cognitive theorists and researchers (Case 1985, Haroutunian 1983, Gardner 1991b) have also challenged Piaget's assertion that the quest for cognitive equilibrium generates the development of new mental structures. We believe that neither his earliest notions of stage theory nor a generalized view of the relationship between the person and his world do much to inform educational practice (see Chapter 7). However, we are still drawn to and have been influenced by his later work. The more Piaget came to understand human growth and development, the less he focused on group-driven conceptions of human cognition and the more he offered to educators. Fosnot (in press) writes of Piaget's later career refinements:

> [Piaget's] theory went through radical reformulation in the ten years prior to his death. In those years he moved away from a simplistic discussion of assimilation, accommodation, and static equilibrium, offering instead a model of dynamic equilibrium characterized by successive coordination and progressive equilibrations. He moved away from a static stage theory (preoperational, concrete, formal) toward a delineation of the successive possibilities and logical necessities generated by subjects as they attempted to explore and understand various problems (p. 7).

Piaget's ground-breaking work spawned an avalanche of theories and research studies, greatly altering cognitive psychology. In our view, the face of what education can be has been changed as well, but educators have not been looking into the mirror.

Discrepancy Resolution

Constructing understandings of one's world is an active, mind-engaging process (Sigel and Cocking 1977, Von Glasersfeld 1981). While it is true that, as learners, we all take in some information passively, the constructivist perspective suggests that even this information must be mentally acted upon in order to have meaning for the learner. Copple, Sigel, and Saunders (1984) highlight the role of discrepancy resolution as perceived by the learner in the construction of knowledge. They discuss the well-known experiment in which a student observes two identical glasses of water filled to the same point and then observes the contents of one glass emptied into a tall, narrow beaker and the contents of the other glass emptied into a short, wide beaker. Young students usually assert that, even though they saw that the amount poured into each of the beakers was identical, the tall, narrow beaker now contains more water than the short, wide one. No amount of teaching, they contend, will alter the students' conceptions. They ask, rhetorically:

> Does the child need to learn to observe the containers more carefully, or perhaps watch more closely when the water is being poured? Does she need to have the water reversed and then repeated until she sees the equivalence (pp. 18)?

Sigel and Cocking (1977) assert that students' fundamental quest is discrepancy resolution. The student who perceives that the two initial glasses held equal amounts of water and the two subsequent beakers did not has no discrepancy with which to contend. In this student's world, defined, in part, by the cognitive structures available to her at that point in time, there is nothing discrepant about equals becoming unequal. However, the student who recognizes that equals must remain equal, even if the receptacles in which they are held change shape, has a discrepancy to resolve. Typically, the discrepancy is resolved by the student incorporating a greater number of variables and new information into her analysis. This is not to say that she will necessarily construct the understanding held by the teacher or other thinkers in the class, just that the new understanding will likely be somewhat more sophisticated than the prior one.

What constitutes sophistication is quite relative and contextual, however. Consider the following example. One cold winter morning, sitting in the car at a red light, a three-year-old child noticed a crossing guard in the intersection walking away from him. The guard was wearing a regulation uniform with the bulky long coat, white gloves, and white, close-fitting hood. In great surprise, the child exclaimed, "Look, there's a snowman crossing the street!" He then added, "I didn't know snowmen were real."

This three-year-old had broadened his "snowman" concept from storybook characters and snowday sculpturing to "real" ones that walk across streets. He experienced cognitive conflict: snow-men aren't alive, but in front of him was one crossing the street. His resolution of the conflict, his more "sophisticated" idea that snowmen are real, which satisfied him at the time, remained until further information and experiences prompted his re-thinking of this understanding. Was this child's "real snowmen" under-standing errant? According to the American College Dictionary (1963, p. 408), errant means "journeying or traveling, as a medieval knight in quest of adventure." In his public radio broadcast, John Lienhard (1993) said, "Five hundred years ago, . . . [a] person in error was a person searching for the truth."

The Need to Find One's Own Problem

Many 8th and 9th graders throughout the nation take algebra. A common problem they are asked to solve is:

> Point A and Point B are 250 miles apart. A train leaves Point A heading for Point B at 11:00 a.m. travelling at 55 MPH, and another train leaves Point B heading for Point A at 11:30 a.m. travelling at 60 MPH. At what time and at what point will they pass one another?

Adults with whom we work still groan at the mention of those trains. As 8th grade students, most of them answered this sort of question correctly on exams because they memorized the appro-priate formal equations and applied them when confronted with the problems. But for most, no new understandings of time and rate functions were constructed, and the equations were quickly forgotten once the exams were completed.

Although designed to foster students' algebraic skills, these types of textbook problems often interfere with students' desire to engage in future mathematical endeavors and, over time, erode students' confidence and self-esteem. The line between cognitive dissonance, which can provoke a student's desire to persevere, and intrapersonal frustration, which interferes with the student's de-sire to resolve dissonance, is a fine one that is often difficult to recognize. To foster the development of students' abilities to organ-ize and understand their individual worlds, teachers need to en-courage students to find their own problems.

29

Coming to know one's world is a function of caring about one's world. Caring about one's world is fostered by communities of learners involved in trying to answer similar, but not necessarily identical, problems. The energy necessary for construction of problem solutions demands commitment. Commitment, in turn, emanates from construction. An engineer watches a newly designed airplane execute a flawless performance and says, "That's my baby!" An architect, after years of long hours working on a blueprint for a complex structure, says, "That's my baby!" A father, at his daughter's black belt karate exhibition says, "That's my baby!" Why the same metaphor? There is a commitment inherent in parenting, an activity that includes design, investment, joy, and pain. Indeed, other activities high in these qualities engender great commitment as well.

Designing, thinking, changing, evaluating—most particularly in response to a felt need—create interest and energy. Cognitive processes work to address affectively driven issues. Helping students or groups of students to clarify for themselves the nature of their own questions, to pose their questions in terms they can pursue, and to interpret the results in light of other knowledge they have generated is the teacher's main task.

The Challenge

Piaget (1969) wrote:

> The heartbreaking difficulty in pedagogy, as, indeed in medicine and in many other branches of knowledge that partake at the same time of art and science, is, in fact, that the best methods are also the most difficult ones: it would be impossible to employ a Socratic method without having first acquired some of Socrates' qualities, the first of which would have to be a certain respect for intelligence in the process of development (p. 69).

A constructivist framework challenges teachers to create environments in which they and their students are encouraged to think and explore. This is a formidable challenge. But to do otherwise is to perpetuate the ever-present behavioral approach to teaching and learning.

References

Bruner, J. (1964). "The Course of Cognitive Growth." *American Psychologist* 19.

Bruner, J. (1986). *Actual Minds, Possible Worlds*. Cambridge, Mass.: Harvard University Press.

Case, R. (1985). *Intellectual Development: Birth to Adulthood*. Orlando, Fla.: Academic Press.

Chomsky, N. (1977). *Language and Responsibility*. New York: Pantheon Books.

Copple, C., I. Sigel, and R. Saunders. (1984). *Educating the Young Thinker*. New York: D. Van Nostrand.

Fosnot, C.T. (in press). "Rethinking Science Education: A Defense of Piagetian Constructivism." *Journal for Research in Science Education*.

Gardner, H. (1991b). *The Unschooled Mind: How Children Think and How Schools Should Teach*. New York: Basic Books.

Haroutunian, S. (1983). *Equilibrium in the Balance*. New York: Springer-Verlag.

Kelly, G.A. (1955). *The Psychology of Personal Constructs*, 2 Vols. (Vol. 1, *A Theory of Personality*; Vol. 2, *Clinical Diagnosis and Psychotherapy*). New York: Norton.

Kuhn, T. (1962). *The Structure of Scientific Revolutions*. Chicago: The University of Chicago Press.

Lienhard, J. (1993). *The Engines of Our Ingenuity, No. 781: Error*. Houston, Texas: National Public Radio, KUHF.

Piaget, J. (1952). *The Origins of Intelligence in Children*. New York: International Universities Press.

Piaget, J. (1969). *The Mechanisms of Perception*. London: Routledge and Keger Paul.

Piaget, J., and B. Inhelder. (1971). *The Psychology of the Child*. N.Y.: Basic Books.

Sigel, I.E., and R.R. Cocking. (1977). *Cognitive Development from Childhood to Adolescence: A Constructivist Perspective*. N.Y.: Holt, Rinehart and Winston.

Skinner, B.F. (1938). *The Behavioral Organism: An Experimental Analysis*. N.Y.: Appleton-Century-Crofts.

Thorndike, E.L. (1926). *The Measurement of Intelligence*. Columbia, New York: Teachers College Press.

Wadsworth, B. (1971). *Piaget's Theory of Cognitive Development; An Introduction for Students of Psychology and Education*. N.Y.: Longman.

von Glasersfeld, E. (1981). "The Concepts of Adaptation and Viability in a Radical Constructivist Theory of Knowledge." In *New Directions in Piagetian Theory and Practice*, edited by I.E. Sigel, Brodinsky, and Golinkoff. Hillsdale, N.J.: Lawrence Erlbaum Associates.

PART II
Some Guiding Principles of Constructivism

Posing Problems of Emerging Relevance to Students

Structuring Learning Around Primary Concepts: The Quest for Essence

Seeking and Valuing Students' Points of View

Adapting Curriculum to Address Students' Suppositions

Assessing Student Learning in the Context of Teaching

4

Posing Problems of Emerging Relevance to Students

One common criticism of constructivism is that, as a pedagogical framework, it subordinates the curriculum to the interests of the child. Critics contend that the constructivist approach stimulates learning only around concepts in which the students have a prekindled interest. Such criticisms miss the mark.

Posing problems of emerging relevance is a guiding principle of constructivist pedagogy. However, relevance does not have to be pre-existing for the student. Not all students arrive at the classroom door interested in learning about verb constructs, motion and mechanics, biological cycles, or historical timelines, but most students can be helped to construct understandings of the importance of these topics. Relevance can emerge through teacher mediation.

In discussing Dewey's notion that education ought to take into account students' interests, Bruner (1971) writes:

> . . . a point of departure is not an itinerary. It is just as mistaken to sacrifice the adult to the child as to sacrifice the child to the adult. It is sentimentalism to assume that the teaching of life can be fitted always to the child's interests just as it is empty formalism to force the child to parrot the formulas of adult society. Interests can be created and stipulated (p. 117).

35

How does a teacher help students consider a topic relevant? First, the teacher should begin with a good problem. For now, let's consider the definition of a good problem-solving situation offered by Joel Greenberg (1990).

> 1. It demands that students make a testable prediction (one preferably testable by the students).
> 2. It makes use of relatively inexpensive equipment. Fancier equipment might be used (to obtain higher precision), but the problem should work well at the low-tech end of the spectrum.
> 3. It is complex enough to elicit multiple problem-solving approaches from the students.
> 4. It benefits from (as opposed to being hindered by) group effort (p. 147).

These criteria are consistent with constructivist pedagogy and speak to both social and cognitive needs in the classroom, whether the students are kindergartners, teenagers, or adults.

We would add a fifth requirement to Greenberg's list. For a situation to be considered a good problem-solving situation in a classroom, at some point, the problem solvers must view the problem as relevant. Problems with little or no initial relevance to students can be made relevant through teacher mediation before or after the problem is posed. For example, it is a rare high school student who independently grapples with the notions of momentum and energy for the intellectual thrill of it. But, with very few exceptions, the following problem of momentum and energy (which meets Greenberg's four criteria) has engaged the diverse groups with whom we have worked.

A set of five hanging pendula with equal size metal balls all touching each other in a resting position is presented to students (see Figure 4.1 on page 37). The teacher raises one ball, releases it, and lets the students note that one ball swings out on the other side. The teacher then raises and releases two balls and the students observe that two balls swing out on the other side. Then the teacher raises three balls and asks the group to predict what will occur when the three balls are released.

We have conducted this lesson with many groups: high school students, college students, school administrators, and teachers of every grade level and subject area. The responses from every group

FIGURE 4.1

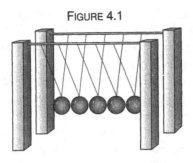

are consistent, and include: (1) one ball will go out, but higher; (2) two balls will go out, but higher; (3) three balls will go out; (4) the balls will "go crazy"; (5) the balls will stop; and (6) the balls will swing together. Some claim that a two-ball swing started by the three ball impact will quickly become a two ball/two ball swing. Some claim that it will result in a two ball/three ball swing. Without exception, at least four of the above responses are articulated by every group; so, without indicating the "right" answer, we always ask the students to explain their responses, react to others' responses, and indicate whether they have changed their minds upon hearing others' predictions. Within a half hour, the groups *demand* that we release the three balls so they can test their theories.

Did any of the people with whom we've shared this activity wake up that morning pondering the variables that affect the swing of a pendulum, or trying to remember the definition of momentum, or considering how both energy and momentum are conserved in the same system? Probably not. In fact, most of the adults with whom we have worked acknowledge that such ponderings have been frightening and alien to them. So why did the apparatus and the questions, for at least the duration of the lesson, prove engaging? What made the problem relevant?

For one thing, the apparatus offers immediate feedback. This feature is a "hook" for many students. But teacher mediation is the key factor. The structuring of the lesson around questions that challenge students' original hypotheses presents students with the initial sparks that kindle their interest. Students must be given time and stimulation to seek relevance and the opportunity to reveal their own points of view. Students need opportunities to ponder the question, form their own responses, and accept the risk of sharing their thoughts with others.

The students' receptiveness toward studying the variables inherent in the pendula apparatus sets the stage for subsequent lessons, the primary aim of which is to encourage students to generate understandings of how to quantify momentum, force, and acceleration, and recognize its existence in other settings. The teacher offers, for example, labs and experiences that focus explicitly on the students' thinking.

To the students who claim that two balls will swing higher when three balls are released, the teacher can assign a lab in which students determine the variables that influence the swing of a pendulum using bobs of different weights and strings of different lengths. The students can then determine how to get a pendulum to swing higher.

To the students who claim that one ball will go out (the typical reason offered is that energy needs a medium through which to travel—in this case, a ball), the teacher can assign a lab in which collisions of different types are examined. Working with steel, clay, and wooden balls, students can design different collisions and reflect on what the outcomes of those collisions might mean.

The students who conserved both momentum and energy in the initial lesson might be asked to consider conservation of momentum beyond those interactions in which the momentum is carried by material objects, such as in the hanging pendula system. What about light? Can momentum be carried by light? This can be a fascinating question, but not necessarily for everyone.

Most high school students, as well as most adults, conceptualize forces in terms of the outcomes that those forces produce. Most students don't understand the conservations and cancellations of forces well enough to make a meaningful inquiry about light arriving on earth from a supernova in space. For other students, such challenges are necessary to maintain an engaging inquiry about momentum. The inquiring teacher mediates the classroom environment in accordance with both the primary concept she has chosen for the class' inquiry and her growing understanding of students' emerging interests and cognitive abilities within the concept.

When posing problems for students to consider and study, it's crucial to avoid isolating the variables *for* the students, to avoid giving them more information than they need or want, and to avoid simplifying the complexity of the problem too early. Complexity often serves to generate relevance and, therefore, interest. It is oversimplification that students find confusing.

Time Versus Coverage

Constructivist teachers often ask students to think about questions they would not ordinarily consider on their own. Of course, highly didactic teachers do the same thing. So what's the difference? A significant difference is that constructivist teachers seek to ask one big question, to give the students time to think about it, and to lead them to the resources to answer it. This is quite different from asking the many specific questions that spring from the prescribed syllabus and, when the questions are not quickly or accurately answered, answering them for the students to keep the pace of the lesson brisk. Most packaged and state- or district-endorsed curriculums have a scope and sequence and fairly rigid timelines. These timelines are not established in service to the intellectual development of the learner. They are created to standardize instructional practices and ensure broad coverage of the whole curriculum.

Constructivist teachers have discovered that the prescribed scope, sequence, and timeline often interferes with their ability to help students understand complex concepts. Rigid timelines are also at odds with research on how human beings form meaningful theories about the ways the world works (Duckworth 1986), how students and teachers develop an appreciation of knowledge and understanding (Eisner 1985), and how one creates the disposition to inquire about phenomena not fully understood (Katz 1985). Most curriculums simply pack too much information into too little time—at a significant cost to the learner.

Teachers everywhere lament how quickly students forget and how little of what they initially remembered they retain over time. Our present curricular structure has engineered that outcome. Students haven't forgotten; they never learned that which we assumed they had. In demanding coverage of a broad landscape of material, we often win the battle but lose the war. We expose students to the material and prepare them for the tests, but we don't allow them to learn the concepts.

The importance of structuring learning opportunities in service to students' concept formation is well-documented (Lochhead 1985, Hunt and Sullivan 1974). If the conceptions presently held by students are not explicitly addressed, new information is filtered through a lens that may cloud, rather than clarify, that information. College students in physics classes might understand notions of quantum mechanics, yet simultaneously hold an Aristotelian view of the forces involved when balls roll down planks or magnets pull on a nail or celestial bodies stay in orbit. This distinction between how individuals construe the "nonschool" world and how they think about school-related notions is also well documented (Perrone 1991, Dykstra et al. 1992, Driver et al. 1985). Why do students have such difficulty transferring, generalizing, and constructing an essential understanding of a subject? Blais (1988), in a discussion of students learning algebra, speaks to an issue that surfaces in every subject area:

> Considered in isolation, conventional instruction appears to be sensible and helpful. But we cannot fairly judge an instructional approach unless we consider what occurs within the novice. The available evidence indicates that novices sabotage good conventional instruction by selecting from it only the minimum necessary to achieve correct, mandated performance. They resist learning anything that is not part of the algorithms they depend on for success. Thus, drawings, estimation, abstraction, connections to simple examples, informal English, learning to read well, and so on, are viewed as unnecessary embellishments. Novices feel they know what is important despite their not perceiving essence. They do not understand shallowness because they do not experience depth (p. 627).

Learning for Transfer

Just as it's important to look for and value the points of view of the students with whom we work, we, as educators, must also look for and value the power of our own perspectives as adults. Doing so both clarifies and complicates. It clarifies our understandings of how people learn and complicates our understandings of how to teach.

It's common for educators to be asked to adopt a new perspective on instruction (for example, to adopt the practice of looking for and valuing the students' points of view) while simultaneously being rebuked for seeking to reconsider assessment practices, management designs, classroom protocols, and the myriad other variables that define teaching and learning. In effect, educators are being told to respond to external stimuli while stifling their own inner perspectives. This fragmented approach to restructuring often creates settings in which contradictory practices co-exist. In attempting to encourage intellectual autonomy, schools often set up elaborate reward and punishment systems to control learning. In attempting to encourage students to appreciate the inter-relatedness of people, phenomena, and ideas, schools offer a series of courses unconnected to one another; for example, science and history classes. We filter out most historical perspectives from science classes because there just isn't enough time to cover even the "science" information. Then, we filter out science from history classes because we have somehow concluded that political wars are more important to study than intellectual leaps. In doing so, we lose sight of our original aims: to encourage students' intellectual development and to foster their acquisition of the skills necessary to serve that purpose.

The fragmentation of the curriculum and the pressures of time have made intellectual inquiry so highly specialized that, by 7th grade, most curriculums are departmentalized and heavily laden with information to be memorized. During their six hours in school each day, students can see seven or eight different teachers, each charged with teaching a different curriculum. Within this structure, students quickly come to perceive knowledge as separate, parallel strands of unrelated information. Many teachers assume that transfer occurs automatically after a sufficient base of information is acquired. Surveys of high school graduates, however, indicate that the information base is short-term and transfer occurs only sporadically (Ravitch and Finn 1987).

41

Learning for transfer is an intellectual activity that must be nurtured and modelled institutionally in schools, classrooms, and families. Too many models of learning are based on assumptions that are found to be faulty year after year for large segments of the student population. Constructivist settings are based on different assumptions and offer new practices. Learning to be a constructivist teacher is important, but not easy. Regular reflection and analysis of personal perspectives on learning help to clarify and assess those perspectives and to align teaching practices in accordance with them.

The Value of Changing One's Mind

The terms "naive beliefs" (McClosky et al. 1980) and "misconceptions" (Lochhead 1988) are used in cognitive research to discuss the idea of helping students "change their minds" about how they interpret the phenomena around them. Changing one's mind is an invaluable element of the learning process. Take the following as an example.

Students in an 8th grade English class put together individual magazines on self-selected topics. The magazine assignment was intended to be interdisciplinary in nature, incorporating a variety of research and writing skills. One student chose the topic of sneakers. He needed help in developing a science-related article for his magazine. Through inquiry and discussion, he and the teacher agreed that a sneaker has to absorb shock, while simultaneously affording a little bounce. It has to grip the road, but not enough to make the wearer trip. The student indicated that how well a sneaker serves these two functions depends on its design, but he did not initially view the materials from which the sneaker was made as affecting those functions. While uncovering the student's point of view, the teacher began to formulate the next day's lesson.

During the next day's class, the teacher convened the "sneakers" investigator, the "racing cars" enthusiast, and the "skateboards" fan. She gave the students two rubber balls and told them that experimenting with the balls may help them put together some thoughts on how sneaker, car, and skateboard manufacturers decide what blends of materials to use in their soles, tires, or

Wheels. The teacher encouraged the students to examine the properties of the two balls. She told them to roll the balls simultaneously down an inclined plane and note what happens.

The balls were the "happy" and "unhappy" balls available from science supply houses. One is made from the widely used synthetic rubber known as neoprene. The other is formed from a proprietary rubber compound developed and manufactured under the trade name Norsorex^{tm}. Although they look almost identical, the balls differ in a number of ways. The students first noticed that one ball (the neoprene) rolls faster. From throwing the ball and missing the catch, they next discovered that the "slow " ball had no bounce. After the students spent about 15 minutes rolling and bouncing the balls, sharing reasons for what was happening, and suggesting terms like "friction," "bounciness," and "force," the teacher rejoined the group to help them consider the notion that blending materials of different attributes can create desired new attributes.

Before this experiment, the students viewed rubber as a singular noun. An item either was rubber or was not. This view changed dramatically. After experimenting, the students were animated in their reformulated ideas that the vast array of sneakers featured in shoe stores and sports shops could also be distinguished by the "bounciness" of materials used in their manufacturing, and that the "bounciness" was not only related to the design, but was a function of the sneaker's material properties as well. The teacher told the group when they were writing up their experiments that there was a "fancy" word for "bounciness." None of them asked what it was. In fact, they continued interrupting her to comment on the "bounciness" of tennis balls, basketballs, and types of racing tires.

This example illustrates only one small area of the students' knowledge base. But it is of interest to note that these three students, in other subject areas and other classes, did not typically address nuance or subtleties in their writing or discourse. It's also interesting to note that none of these students considered this topic relevant at the unit's onset. In many aspects of their thinking, they exhibited an "either/or" frame of reference. The relevance emerged for these students initially through the teacher's mediation of the task and subsequently through their own desire to solve what Greenberg (1990) calls "a good problem."

* * *

The notion of emerging relevance was one of our first generated universals—or what we call guiding principles— of constructivist teaching. As we studied this principle, we realized that the nature of questions posed to students greatly influences the depth to which the students search for answers. Posing problems of emerging relevance and searching for windows into students' thinking form a particular frame of reference about the role of the teacher and about the teaching process. It cannot be included in a teacher's repertoire as an add-on. It must be a basic element of that repertoire.

References

Blais, D.M. (November 1988). "Constructivism: A Theoretical Revolution for Algebra." *Mathematics Teacher* 624-631.

Bruner, J. (1971). *The Relevance of Education*. N.Y.: Norton.

Driver, R., E. Guesne, and A. Tiberghien, eds. (1985). *Children's Ideas in Science*. Philadelphia: Open University Press.

Duckworth, E. (November 1986). "Teaching as Research." *Harvard Educational Review* 56, 4: 481-495.

Dykstra, D., Jr., C.F. Boyle, and I.A. Monarch. (1992). "Studying Conceptual Change in Learning Physics." *Science Education* 76, 6: 615-652.

Eisner, E., ed. (1985). "Aesthetic Modes of Knowing." *Learning and Teaching the Ways of Knowing, 84th Yearbook of the National Society for the Study of Education*. Chicago: University of Chicago Press, pp. 23-36.

Forman, G., and P.B. Pufall, eds. *Constructivism in the Computer Age*. Hillsdale, N.J.: Lawrence Erlbaum Associates.

Greenberg, J. (1990). *Problem-Solving Situations, Volume I*. Grapevine Publications, Inc.

Hunt, D.E., and E.V. Sullivan. (1974). *Between Psychology and Education*. Hinsdale, Ill.: The Dryden Press.

Katz, L.G. (1985). "Dispositions in Early Childhood Education." *ERIC/EECE Bulletin* 18, 2. Urbana, Ill.: ERIC Clearinghouse on Elementary and Early Childhood Education.

Lochhead, J. (1985). "New Horizons in Educational Development." *Review of Research in Education*. Washington, D.C.: American Educational Research Association.

Lochhead, J. (1988). "Some Pieces of the Puzzle." In *Constructivism in the Computer Age*, edited by G. Forman and P. Pufall. Hillsdale, N.J.: Lawrence Erlbaum Associates.

McClosky, M., A. Caramazza, and B. Green. (December 1980). "Curvilinear Motions in the Absence of External Forces: Naive Beliefs About the Motion of Objects." *Science* 210: 1139-1141.

Perrone, V. (1991). *A Letter to Teachers*. San Francisco: Jossey Bass.

Ravitch, D., and C. Finn. (1987). *What Do Our 17-Year-Olds Know?: A Report on the First National Assessment of History and Literature*. New York: Harper & Row.

5

Principle #2

Structuring Learning Around Primary Concepts: The Quest for Essence

Structuring curriculum around primary concepts is a critical dimension of constructivist pedagogy. When designing curriculum, constructivist teachers organize information around conceptual clusters of problems, questions, and discrepant situations because students are most engaged when problems and ideas are presented holistically rather than in separate, isolated parts. Much of traditional education breaks wholes into parts and then focuses separately on each part. But many students are unable to build concepts and skills from parts to wholes. These students often stop trying to see the wholes before all the parts are presented to them and focus on the small, memorizable aspects of broad units without ever creating the big picture. Think, for example, of assembling a bicycle. The package contains precise written directions in sequential order, but most of us continually refer to the picture of the bicycle on the box. We need to see the "whole" before we are able to make sense of the parts.

In the now-defunct Chicago Mastery Learning System, reading was presented to students as approximately 300 discrete skills to be mastered in sequential order. Most skills came with their own tests for mastery. Students worked on each skill in sequence until it was mastered. In such arrangements, the forest gets obscured by the trees, and each separate skill becomes its own whole to be mastered. Some students are able to master individual reading skills without becoming very proficient readers while some competent readers have a difficult time with the separate skills. In other words, the part-to-whole approach is not necessarily predictive of student success.

When concepts are presented as wholes, on the other hand, students seek to make meaning by breaking the wholes into parts that *they* can see and understand. Students initiate this process to make sense of the information; they construct the process and the understanding rather than having it done *for* them. With curricular activities clustered around broad concepts, students can select their own unique problem-solving approaches and use them as springboards for the construction of new understandings. In a high school social studies class, for example, a teacher structured a unit on conflict around three conflicts involving American troops: the Revolutionary War, the Civil War, and World War II. The teacher wrote the names of the three wars on the chalkboard and then asked students to reflect on what they already knew about these wars, to select two of the three wars, and to compare them by illustrating their similarities and differences.

Rather than presenting facts to the students about each of the three wars, the teacher chose an activity that encouraged students to reflect, analyze, compare, and contrast. He created a setting in which students could learn facts from each other and their text-book *while* constructing their own new conceptual understandings of the broader theme of conflict. One student interpreted the Revolutionary War and the Civil War as wars fought to achieve freedom, while seeing World War II as a war fought to protect it. Another student differentiated between the Civil War and the other two wars by focusing on the nationality of the soldiers: the Civil War pitted American against American. A third student reported that the colors of the uniforms worn by soldiers during the Revolutionary War and World War II were different. She thought that they would have been the same, since she noted the flag had changed design, but not colors.

All three students responded to the task, but are their responses examples of bits of information or are they examples of newly constructed knowledge? The students' facial expressions, tones of surprise, and pauses while engaging in the task suggested that they were student constructions. This "material" could have been "covered" in a lecture. But, in that case, the new understandings wouldn't have been "aha's" at all. They likely would have become new bits of information in a long string of previously disseminated bits.

Conceptual Clusters

Let's look briefly at two other approaches to structuring curriculum around primary concepts. First, the National Center for Improving Science Education, after considerable deliberation over what is important in science education for adolescents, generated a list of "conceptual themes": cause and effect, change and conservation, diversity and variation, energy and matter, evolution and equilibrium, models and theories, probability and prediction, structure and function, systems and interaction, and time and scale (Bybee et al. 1989). These themes represent the Center's quest for essence in science education—the "big ideas" of science.

As a second example, Melchior (1992), a junior high school principal on Long Island, discusses structuring curriculum around concepts that twig student reflection. He identifies them as "polar conflicts" and invites students to reflect on their relationships. The list of concepts includes: independence/interdependence/dependence; impulsivity/reflection; individual/group; fantasy/realism; freedom/responsibility; reactive/proactive; inhumanity/ sensitivity; chaos/cosmos; objective/subjective; and static/dynamic. Teachers in the school select and use these conflicts in exploring the curriculum. An 8th grade English teacher, for example, used the fantasy/reality dichotomy to engage her students in a discussion of Poe's "The Tell Tale Heart," while a physical education teacher selected the impulsivity/reflection dichotomy to initiate discussions about sportsmanship. These polar conflicts can be applied in all subject areas, serving as the "big ideas" around which explorations of content-specific topics are woven. These explorations create opportunities for students to structurally shift their thinking about the phenomena around them. The facts that accompany topics become more relevant for students once the students become engaged in reflection on the big concepts.

Learners of all ages are more engaged by concepts introduced by the teacher and constructed by the learner from whole-to-part, rather than part-to-whole. It's more effective, for example, to permit budding writers to invent their own spelling and publish their material for others to read and for themselves to re-read than to teach the rules of grammar and conventional spelling and then ask students to put the skills together in an original piece of writing. Problems structured around "big ideas" provide a context in which students learn component skills, gather information, and build knowledge. Attempts to linearize concept formation quickly stifle the learning process.

Who's in Charge of Learning?

We are all responsible for our own learning. The teacher's responsibility is to create educational environments that permit students to assume the responsibility that is rightfully and naturally theirs. Teachers do this by encouraging self-initiated inquiry, providing the materials and supplies appropriate for the learning tasks, and sensitively mediating teacher/student and student/student interactions. But, the teacher cannot take sole responsibility for the students' learning.

In a recent survey of resident undergraduates at a large state university, students reported that their areas of least growth were "changing views," "writing," and "mathematical ability" (Ludwig 1992, p. 24). The areas in which they reported having grown the most were "meeting new and different people", "making decisions independently," "leadership," and "social confidence." Although the differences at first seem startling, they are really quite predictable. Resident life necessitates the construction of one's own role in the new social order of dormitories. The environment requires independence. Because students are responsible for their own socialization, they mature in this area. But, in traditional academic domains, the instructor determines what is to be learned, how it is to be learned, and the pace and rhythm of the learning. The learner, to a large degree, loses control. With someone else in charge, personal growth diminishes.

"Less is more" is an underlying theme of *Science for All Americans* (AAAS 1989). This theme is an important notion for teachers to explore. It provocatively encourages re-organization of concepts and information. Teachers can enhance the likelihood of student learning by decreasing the number of facts and specific bits of information they want students to "cover." Through reflection on and attention to the primary concepts teachers have culled from their own experiences, they can provide materials and questions that guide students in identifying their own concepts.

We now provide two detailed examples of curriculum designed around some "big ideas": the conceptual themes of classification and of positive and negative space.

Conceptual Theme: Classification

At a conference a few years ago, we learned of an activity Ralph Adams designed for his chemistry class at the Vernon-Verona-Sherrill High School in New York State. We adapted this activity to illustrate the guiding principles of constructivism and have used it in college-level teacher preparation programs and K-12 inservice staff development workshops.

In this activity, small groups of participants examine a list of 95 book titles, each with a classification name and a number, and arrange the books on a seven-shelf bookcase with space for thirty-two books per shelf, according to a given set of rules (see the example in Figure 5.1 on p. 51).

The rules for the activity are that (1) the books must be grouped vertically by their classification names, and (2) the books must be placed on the shelves in consecutive order horizontally. The students quickly get to work, frequently clarifying the instructions with the teacher or facilitator when they find that the task is not as easy as it originally appears. The groups work independently for over one hour.

Some groups cut the five pages of book titles into strips and work with those strips as they spread them out over the tabletops and across the floor. Other groups focus on the book numbers and work directly on the book shelf, asking for more shelves as they repeatedly change their approach. Other groups seek mathematical relationships among the book numbers and the number of books in each classification, and they delay the task of putting the books on the shelves until they can generate some predictable patterns. It's interesting to note that each group's investment in its approach is usually so strong that there is virtually no peering

FIGURE 5.1

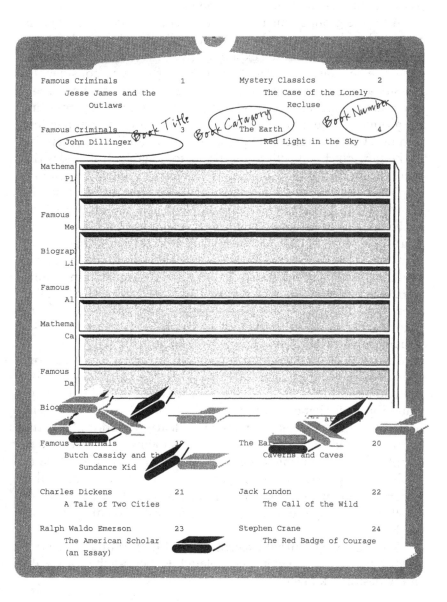

around the room; and when one group completes the task, the other groups do not seek their help. Each group simply wants time to finish their arrangement of the books.

After the groups finish the activity with the books, the task is re-introduced as a metaphor for the periodic table of elements. Though the students aren't explicitly given the metaphor ahead of time, the new task provides them an opportunity to consider the classificatory nature of the periodic table. The metaphor emerges. The books represent the periodic elements; the numbers represent the atomic numbers, and the classifications represent the chemical families. Consider an example: the Group O Family of elements is at the far right-hand column of the periodic table. It includes the inert gases: helium, neon, argon, krypton, xenon, and radon, originally thought to be nonreactive, stable elements that do not combine with any other elements to form compounds. Let's look at the book titles associated with these elements. The book classification is Mystery Classics, somewhat reminiscent of the mysterious quality of the inert gases, which are not often found in nature. Book 2, *The Case of the Lonely Recluse*, is helium, with an atomic number of 2. Helium *is* a recluse. Helium atoms always exist separately. They are never part of a molecule, nor do they form compounds. Book 10, *Red Light at Dawn*, is element 10, neon, which glows bright red when high-voltage electricity is passed through it. Book 18, *A Bulb Broke at Midnight*, is element 18, argon, the gas in an ordinary lightbulb. The puns, references to everyday life and literature, and unusual descriptions of the elements continue for each element in the periodic table. This lesson consistently generates enormous interest in learning more about the properties and characteristics of the elements, a subject many people may find intimidating or may not find initially relevant. With so many references to literature and history, the lesson also generates laments from participants who claim that they are not "well-read" enough, but who express interest in reading some of the books.

The following journal excerpt (Hees 1992) from a preservice science teacher who had just completed the bookshelf task speaks of the desire to know more:

> My most persistent thought: Among the four of us future science teachers, we knew virtually nothing about the proper-

ties of the elements. We have no basic familiarity with the elements—what they look like, what they smell like, their state at room temperature, their particular uses in industry.

We were adept at maneuvering symbols, but symbols for what? We knew little about them. What little we did know was mostly second-hand information. It struck me that you could lay 94 different elemental blocks in front of me, and I could positively identify perhaps five to ten. While not a chemist, I don't think I'm comparatively ignorant in the subject either. Somewhere along the way in our education we should be allowed to experience the pure *stuff* out of which everything is made. When we learn the periodic table, it would then be a table of elements, not a table of symbols.

The question arises: are not the books in the above example just another set of symbols the students are expected to maneuver? The students arrange a large number of books, a task that, in some small way, offers them the chance to recapitulate aspects of the experiences well-known chemists had while piecing together the periodic laws of nature. Many adults with whom we have shared this activity admit that although they managed to pass chemistry classes, they never understood the classificatory nature of the periodic table. They were simply told to memorize it. As adults, in the context of trying to better understand constructivist pedagogy, they have re-acquainted themselves with a former field of study and for the first time have begun to see order in something that was inaccessible in earlier years. These revelations illustrate for them the importance of structuring learning around "big ideas."

The following journal entry (Ferrandino 1991) from another preservice teacher illustrates the type of thinking that open-ended activities focused on "big ideas" can foster:

I have to admit that as much as I came to appreciate the exercise of re-creating, so to speak, the periodic table of elements, I found it difficult to initially become engaged by this task. At first glance it seemed overwhelming and without purpose (although I should have known better!). Fortunately, my group partners attacked the problem right away and I was just content to observe their progress. They decided to list each category. Next to each category/subject, the book numbers that belonged to each category were listed in ascending order. Very quickly they decided to look for a "formula" that might describe the sequence of books in each category. To my amazement, their hunch was correct and we quickly established a means to predict the numerical sequence for any category. I still don't know why they even suspected such a sequence might exist, but it did, and we found it quickly. At this point I was simultaneously engaged and distracted because I noticed the sequence involved adding 2, 8, 18, and 32 to previous book numbers to obtain the next book number in the series. These I recognized as the maximum number of electrons permitted to occupy each shell of an atom. I was distracted by trying to re-create the expression that generates this series as well as the series that predicts the maximum number of electrons allowable in each subshell.

In order to understand, students must search for meaning. In order to search for meaning, students must have the opportunity to form and ask questions. Flannery (1991) quotes Arbor, who states that:

> . . . a metaphor is good and useful as long as its imperfections are kept in mind. The imperfections are the dissimilarities that exist between the principal and subsidiary subjects. Despite dangers, these imperfections are important to the functioning of metaphors because "it is their imperfections which set them in the boundary region of scientific thought where they can exercise their unique power of acting as connecting links with other worlds of experience."

Most adults can make the connection between books organized to fit onto shelves to convey their thematic relationships, and elements organized in a symbolic array to convey their chemical relationships. The metaphor need not be "perfect" to be a good teaching tool. In fact, as the learners search to measure the "fit" between the bookshelf and the periodic table, they ask critical questions about the study of chemistry, and they form provisional answers. They learn that the periodic table of elements is a carefully crafted method of classifying the elements that comprise our physical world. They also learn that it's not the only method.

Conceptual Theme: Positive and Negative Space

Curriculums can be designed around conceptual themes in all types of classes at all grade levels. The next example is from a middle school art class. It's an example of a teacher-directed set of lessons. The class was a heterogeneous mix of 7th and 8th grade students. The "drawing negative space" unit was designed to enhance students' abilities to look at and draw three-dimensional objects from different perspectives. "Positive space" is the name given to the space taken up by an object. "Negative space" is the name given to the space around the object. For example, Figure 5.2 illustrates the two different sketches that can be drawn of a triangle. In picture 1, the positive space has been thatched. In picture 2, the negative space has been thatched.

FIGURE 5.2

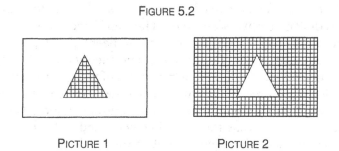

PICTURE 1   PICTURE 2

Activity 1. The first activity in this unit asked students to draw simple shapes that connect to the edge of the paper. Then, they cut out the space around the shape and placed it on a paper of a contrasting color. Students found that the first shape can be redrawn by drawing the negative shape. This phenomenon occurs because positive and negative spaces share edges. In this activity, the students were not asked to see the negative space before they drew it. The concepts of negative and positive space were only discussed and explored after the students had produced the product. Figure 5.3 illustrates three examples of students' work.

FIGURE 5.3

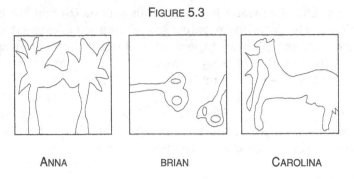

ANNA   BRIAN   CAROLINA

Activity 2. Next, the teacher asked the students to look through a viewfinder at a wooden stool. The viewfinder was a piece of construction paper with a rectangular peephole of proportions identical to the paper. The students held their viewfinders so that the stool touched its edges at a minimum of two points. They were then asked to direct their gazes at one negative space until they could see it, as they had done with the cut-out shapes. They were asked to imagine that the stool vanished and only the negative spaces remained. When the students drew the shapes of the spaces, the object was inadvertently drawn, but with greater ease because the students were facing only one problem at a time—what they saw, not what they "knew." The three drawings in Figure 5.4 represent some student responses.

FIGURE 5.4

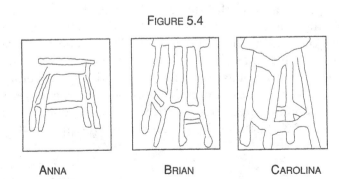

ANNA   BRIAN   CAROLINA

Activity 3. The teacher then assigned a new task of drawing negative space by setting up a plant and asking the students to look at it through the same viewfinder. The teacher, once again, asked the students to gaze at the spaces surrounding the object until those spaces took shape. Then, the students drew the spaces around the plant.

FIGURE 5.5

ANNA	BRIAN	CAROLINA

These sets of drawings document the students' progress in looking at objects from various perspectives and recognizing differences. The lessons the teacher designed invited students to look at boundaries from multiple perspectives, a skill that spills over into social studies discussions, geometric principles, and the domain of art and design, among others.

The first two activities minimized the number of variables the students had to consider. The first task didn't ask students to see negative space. It simply helped students categorize negative space and positive space. Thus, the primary cognitive demand of the lesson was one of classification. In the second activity the students focused on negative space, but the viewfinder limited the complexity of the task by defining and limiting the negative space. In chapter 4, we asked educators *not* to reduce the complexity of issues prematurely for students. What's the difference in this example? Here, the teacher wanted the students to consider the concept of perspective without struggling with the frustrations many students experience when attempting to "capture reality" in two dimensions on paper. The teacher wanted to minimize the students' evaluation of their own drawing "competence" and focus their energies on exploring the concept of perspective. Being contained in the viewfinder, negative space approximated the characteristics of positive space. Such an approximation helped the students begin to see negative space as if it were positive space, a perspective that the teacher found helpful in informing the middle school students' perspective-taking abilities.

These activities require *decentration*, the cognitive acknowledgment that one's own view is not the only one nor necessarily the "correct" one, but is one of many. It's interesting to note that the students who found activities 2 and 3 "boring" and "no fun" were students who, in other activities, evidenced a limited ability to decenter. A teacher listening carefully can use such comments when designing future activities.

The Chance to See More

Structuring curriculum around "big ideas" and broad concepts provides multiple entry points for students: some become engaged through practical responses to problems, some analyze tasks based on models and principles, and others interpret ideas through metaphors and analogies from their unique perspectives. The environment and the use of broad concepts invite each student to participate irrespective of individual styles, temperaments, and dispositions.

Student engagement is a function of many variables, two of which are one's interest in the topic and one's perception of personal competence. An idea won't automatically engage students simply because it is "big." Classification, as we have discussed, is a "big idea." However, presenting classification as a ditto that requires students to group items by their initial consonant sound trivializes the concept and contributes little to the development of understanding. The teacher's ability to foster collegial interaction among students, mediate the emergence of relevance, and match curricular questions to the student's present suppositions encourages the student's search for understanding.

References

American Association for the Advancement of Science. (1989). *Science for All Americans*. Washington, D.C.: AAAS.

Bybee, R., C. Buchwald, S. Crissman, D. Heil, P. Kuerbis, C. Matsumoto, and J. McInerney. (1989). *Science and Technology Education for the Elementary Years: Frameworks for Curriculum and Instruction*. Andover, Mass.: The National Center for Improving Science Education.

Ferrandino, F. (1991). Unpublished manuscript. New York: SUNY at Stony Brook.

Flannery, M.C. (1991). *Bitten by the Biology Bug: Essays from The American Biology Teacher*. Reston, Va.: National Association of Biology Teachers.

Hees, B. (1992). Unpublished manuscript. New York: SUNY at Stony Brook.

Ludwig, J. (September 1992). "Closing the Gap: Getting and Using Feedback from Students." In *Assessment at SUNY: Principles, Process, and Case Studies*. Stony Brook, N.Y.: University Faculty Senate: SUNY Central Administration.

Melchior, T. (Summer 1992). "The Disparate Nature of Learning Or Team Teaching Is Not Enough." *Teaching Thinking and Problem Solving*. Philadelphia: Research for Better Schools 14, 3.

6

Seeking and Valuing Students' Points of View

Seeking to understand students' points of view is essential to constructivist education. The more we study the learning process, the more we understand how fundamental this principle is. Students' points of view are windows into their reasoning. Awareness of students' points of view helps teachers challenge students, making school experiences both contextual and meaningful. Each student's point of view is an instructional entry point that sits at the gateway of personalized education. Teachers who operate without awareness of their students' points of view often doom students to dull, irrelevant experiences, and even failure. Hunt and Sullivan (1974) state:

> If an educational system has only universal goals and a limited variety of educational approaches, it is not surprising that the results for many students will end in failure. This is because these students did not fit the system. It is not entirely the students who are fixed and unchangeable; it is also the system (p. 45).

We have all been to workshops or meetings in which the presenter has begun the session by asking the participants what they hope to learn or accomplish. Often, people's responses are made into a list on the board. Then the presenter starts the session and never again refers to the list. This might be an example of looking for the students' points of view, but it's definitely not an example of valuing them. Valuing students' points of view means not only recognizing them but also addressing them.

Acknowledging Relativity

In a philosophical sense, the notion of relativity is embedded within the search to understand another person's point of view. The acknowledgement that other perspectives exist implies relativity of importance and merit, and casts doubt on some of the many other "truths" we often accept without reflection. A good example of multiple perspectives can be found in almost any faculty lounge in almost any school in America. Think about the faculty lounge in your school, about what happens there and about the significance various occupants attach to those happenings. The following journal entry (Schlopp 1993) is from a young woman preparing to become a teacher.

> Mr. Feldman greeted me and brought me to the teachers' lounge. To me, this was always a sacred place where I was never allowed to go as a child. I still felt I didn't belong there. I was 10 years old all over again. The teachers' lounge was a place of mystery, and now that mystery was about to unfold before my eyes. It was not at all what I expected. There was furniture left over from the 1960s with some really bad curtains. Teachers were there complaining about some students. One teacher had a student throw-up in class, and all were complaining about the student who pulled a fire alarm. There were a few teachers actually playing cards. The pledge of allegiance came on the loud speaker and it felt so weird not to stand up, but I fought the urge and just sat there.

That faculty lounge on a chilly winter morning in February was an unfolding mystery to this preservice teacher. It's unlikely that any other occupant there that day perceived the room's events in the same manner. This individuality of perception and meaning is repeated over and over again with students in every classroom in the school. Ms. Scholpp shares another story about differing perspectives:

> In college I was an environmental science major, and for my field biology final I had to learn 100 bird calls. I listened to

that tape morning, noon, and night. My roommate was a nursing major and thought the whole thing was stupid. (I was driving her crazy.) Everything is relevant from someone else's point of view.

The Teacher's Role: Talking *and* Listening

When we think of the teacher's role, most individuals evoke an image of someone talking and passing on information to someone else. "Getting information across" is viewed as a teacher's primary responsibility. While it is certainly true that virtually all teachers do a good deal of talking to and with their students, listening is at least an equally important component of a constructivist teacher's repertoire. Let's explore a kindergarten classroom to see why.

It was the middle of March. In this kindergarten class, as in most kindergarten classes throughout the nation, the middle of March means the appearance of green construction paper and pictures of leprechauns. The task on this particular day was to cut out the ten numbered leprechauns from the ditto sheet and paste them on the green paper in consecutive numerical order. One little boy, Nicholas, began the project in the following manner:

FIGURE 6.1

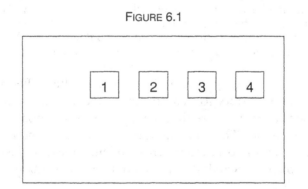

He continued in the typical left-to-right, top-to-bottom fashion.

FIGURE 6.2

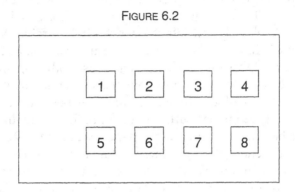

After placing the first eight leprechauns in two evenly spaced rows, he had two leprechauns left over but no room on the green paper to begin a third row. After a moment's thought, he solved his problem in the following manner:

FIGURE 6.3

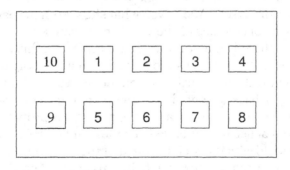

The next day the teacher returned Nicholas' paper to him with the word, "backwards," written on it. When Nicholas went home, he asked his mother what the word on the green paper meant. When his mother told him, Nicholas looked surprised. "It's not backwards," he said. He pointed and counted, "1, 2, 3, 4, 5, 6, 7, 8. Then I didn't have any room, so I did 9 and 10." Nicholas' mother suggested that he take the paper back to his teacher and explain his reasoning. The next morning, however, Nicholas took the paper out of his backpack and left it on the kitchen table. When his mother asked him why he wasn't taking it to school, he shrugged and said he didn't want to take it. When his mother again encouraged him to do so, Nicholas said, "No. It doesn't make a difference." He bounded out of the house toward the bus stop and didn't mention the green paper with the ten leprechauns again.

When he said that bringing the paper back to the teacher didn't make a difference, we don't know what aspect of the situation Nicholas had in mind. Was the whole assignment not worth further discussion from his perspective? Was trying to explain his point of view not "worth it"? We don't know.

Of course, we also don't know what the teacher had in mind when she wrote the word "backwards" on the green paper. Did the teacher think that writing "backwards" on his paper was going to help him seriate the numbers "better" or "correctly" the next time? Because Nicholas did not yet read independently, did she think that her comment was going to generate a discussion between parent and child at home that would help Nicholas learn the left-to-right, top-to-bottom, in-consecutive-order format used in reading readiness programs? For whom did she write the comment—Nicholas, his parents, or herself? And, given what she saw on the paper, what are her own conceptions of the word "backwards"?

Clearly, there is much thinking underpinning this interaction that eludes us. The teacher's motives in giving the assignment and writing the word "backwards" and Nicholas' reasons for not bringing the paper back to school are unknown to us. However, we do know that Nicholas learned a lesson, and it was probably not the lesson the teacher had intended. The lesson he probably learned has more to do with the social context of the classroom. And if that lesson is repeated often enough in this and other classrooms, Nicholas will soon learn that articulating and defending his own point of view is not as valued as ferreting out and reciting back the teacher's point of view.

Also, in this case, the judgment the teacher reached about Nicholas' reasoning was based on suppositions that turned out to be faulty. Let's look at one response that might have confirmed or denied the teacher's suppositions and may have served Nicholas better. The teacher might have asked the beautifully simple question: "Can you tell me how you put these leprechauns in this order?" She may have discovered Nicholas' initial reasoning and also offered him the option of rethinking his initial ideas. Had she done this, Nicholas could have been challenged to re-examine his work, an important activity in his cognitive development—an activity that depends on the teacher's willingness to ask good questions and listen.

Opportunities to Express One's Point of View

We don't intend to minimize the enormous task of the teacher by implying that every utterance or artifact rendered by a student can be given careful attention. They cannot. Seeking students' points of view is an often paradoxical endeavor. The timing and content of teachers' mediations greatly affects the willingness of students to reveal their thinking.

So how do teachers maximize opportunities for students to express their points of view, to reveal their conceptions, to reflect on their conceptions, and to grow intellectually? Teachers' ability to uncover students' conceptions is, to a large degree, a function of the questions and problems posed to students. For example, asking students to place the four seasons in chronological order beginning with winter will elicit a different set of responses than asking students "Why are there seasons?" The first task will help the teacher judge if the students know the "right" answer to the specific question asked. But, sometimes, as in Nicholas' case, even the "right" may be obscured. The second task will likely provide a window into the students' conceptions of the earth's rotations, revolutions, and distance from and angle in relationship to the sun.

Different types of curricular problems give rise to different types of student responses and classroom interactions. If the teacher's quest is coverage of the curriculum in preparation for a multiple-choice test, perhaps the first task will serve that purpose more directly. However, if student understanding is the teacher's quest, the second task will be more significant in assessing those understandings and structuring ensuing activities.

Asking Students to Elaborate

It's important to note that most students have been trained to view both a teacher's asking for elaboration and a teacher's challenge to their ideas as sure signs that their responses are incorrect. Generally speaking, a teacher asks a second question of a student only when she considers the first response incorrect. Because of this, both the challenging of ideas and the seeking of elaboration automatically threaten students. However, when these two practices become a regular classroom custom, students overcome their ingrained aversion to the dreaded second question, and come to understand that the teacher is genuinely interested in knowing more about what they think and why.

In a 6th grade classroom, a group of students were studying buoyancy. Sitting around a tub of water, the teacher held a paper clip in one hand and a plastic unifix cube in the other. She gave the two items to one student, Jane, and asked the others to predict what would happen when Jane dropped them both into the water. Bob quickly indicated that the unifix cube would float and the paper clip would sink. The teacher said, "Tell us why you think that." Bob then immediately changed his prediction and said that the paper clip would float and the cube would sink. The teacher responded, "Please tell us why you think *that*." The teacher had challenged both of Bob's responses, and he was now thoroughly confused. He looked to her and asked, "Which one is it?" She asked, "What do you think?" He thought for a moment and then, returning to his initial hypothesis, explained why he thought that the paper clip would sink (it was made of metal) and why he thought the cube would float (it was made of plastic). After Jane released the items, Bob saw that his initial impulse had been accurate. The teacher asked Bob if he thought the same result would occur if he were to repeat what Jane had just done. He said, "Yes. I think so. Let me try."

The teacher's follow-up question to Bob's "correct" response had made him abandon his initial perspective. Her follow-up question to his second response led him to rethink the whole issue and, equally importantly, reveal his point of view. The teacher now had information about the variables he considered when thinking about buoyancy.

What Really Counts?

A community newspaper recently ran a series of articles relating to a survey conducted at the local high school. Many people in the community are concerned about what is described in these articles as "rampant cheating." The first survey question for the high school students was worded: "Have you ever copied a homework assignment that counted?" It is interesting that the survey developers were specifically interested in the homework that "counted." One is left to wonder which homework "counts" and which homework doesn't, and how students come to know the difference. From our perspective, it would be interesting to find out why students would copy homework that doesn't "count" and why teachers would assign such work. Focusing so much attention on cheating and counting certainly has the potential to divert attention from the processes of teaching and learning. And aren't teaching and learning what really "count"?

Focusing on whether or not students are aware of certain information, or can compute with certain algorithms, or can recite certain verses, implies a linear model of knowledge building. In this model, there is little reason to ask for students' points of view because their points of view are not as valued as are their "right" or "wrong" answers. But knowledge is not linear, nor is the process of learning. Learning is a journey, not a destination. Each point of view is a temporary intellectual stop along the path of ever-increasing knowledge.

Students try to "steal" others' points of view because schools have somehow subordinated the formation of concepts and the building of ideas to high-stakes games of "right" and "wrong" answers that produce winners and losers. The system itself gives students the message that it's better to be "right" than to have interesting ideas. Faced with this sort of pressure, many students—

97 percent by their own acknowledgement, more than most people in our community expected—choose to copy.

We're not condoning cheating, but we do think it's important for educators to explore the dynamics of a system that places so much emphasis on "rightness" and "wrongness." On most tests and homework assignments, students aren't asked to reveal and elaborate on their points of view. They are asked instead to be "right." Being "right" often diverts energy away from the generation of new views. We must remember that the Ptolemaic view of the solar system was a conceptual stop on a path that led to the Copernican views presently held by most astronomers. We think today that Ptolemy was not "right," but his point of view certainly counted.

References

Hunt, D.E., and E.V. Sullivan. (1974). *Between Psychology and Education.* Hinsdale, Ill.: The Dryden Press.

Schlopp, K. (1993). Unpublished manuscript. New York: SUNY at Stony Brook.

7

Principle #4

Adapting Curriculum To Address Students' Suppositions

Learning is enhanced when the curriculum's cognitive, social, and emotional demands are accessible to the student. Therefore, some sort of relationship must exist between the demands of the curriculum and the suppositions that each student brings to a curricular task. This notion leads us to our fourth guiding principle of constructivist teaching: the need for teachers to adapt curriculum tasks to address students' suppositions. If suppositions are not explicitly addressed, most students will find lessons bereft of meaning, regardless of how charismatic the teacher or attractive the materials might be.

Over the years, our view of this guiding principle of constructivist teaching has evolved. The roots of our understandings of constructivism took hold in the idea of matching the curriculum's cognitive demands to students' cognitive abilities. Our initial conception of this process was somewhat linear: if the successful completion of a curricular task required, for example, students to conserve discontinuous quantity, and the students in the class were not yet able to do so, we felt that the task ought not be given. We have come to realize, however, that requiring a one-to-one match between the cognitive demands of curricular tasks and students' cognitive abilities (as we perceive them) can be limiting for students, and can result in the failure of schools to expose students to appropriately challenging concepts.

Addressing Suppositions

A brief history of this principle's derivation illustrates its centrality to creating constructivist classrooms. The seminal works of Jean Piaget formed the framework on which we based the foundational premise of this principle. Piaget observed patterns in the development of his own children's reasoning and then observed and reported the same patterns in other young children. As his own children grew, he also reported consistencies in older children's responses to intellectual tasks. These patterns have been supported by many other scholars and researchers (Inhelder, Sinclair, and Bovet 1974; Elkind 1974; Sigel and Cocking 1977; Wadsworth 1978; and Lowery 1974 a, b, c). In brief, Piaget and others postulate that at different periods, children use different mental structures to think about and make sense of their world. The structures available to children are determined by their biological readiness and life experiences.

Piaget's most widely known conceptualization of cognitive development identifies four stages at which mental structures appear to emerge: (1) the sensorimotor period, the period between birth and about two years when the infant learns by physically acting on the environment and accommodating new schemes, learning that objects have constant shapes and that bodily movements can be coordinated with other objects; (2) the preoperational period, the period roughly between the ages of two and seven years, when the child learns language and other forms of representation, and begins to relate objects and ideas to one another in time and space; (3) the concrete operational period, the period roughly between the ages of 7 and 11 years, when the child's reasoning processes broaden to include what is known as logic, but logic mostly in terms of what is tangible and observable; and (4) the formal operational period, the period that begins sometime during or beyond adolescence, when an individual can use abstract logical structures in diverse problem areas.

At first blush, Piaget's stage theory places into context much of what we see students do in school. Even more compelling are Piaget's ideas in combination with other theories of development, such as Erikson's (1950) conceptualizations of the psycho-social dilemmas we encounter at different times of our lives, Elkind's

(1970) explanations of cognitive conquests, Kohlberg's (1969) notions of male moral development, and Gilligan's (1982) extension of Kohlberg's work highlighting how females respond to moral dilemmas and choices. These theories, together with Piaget's work, add much richness to our observations and understandings of developing human beings.

But ultimately, as we indicate in Chapter 3, stage theories don't prove to be very helpful in explaining the relationship between teaching and learning. In fact, a superficial understanding of stage theory gives teachers little more than new labels to use when describing students. A child can easily become known as "only concrete operational," and be viewed as incapable of learning much from an activity designed, for example, to generate reasons why certain objects float. But a child does not have to demonstrate, a priori, the ability to engage in proportional reasoning to be able to learn by observing floating or sinking objects in a pool of water and generalizing rules to explain what he sees.

Categorizing students' general abilities does not help teachers in developing appropriate instructional strategies for particular topics and concepts because at any one point in time, people use several different cognitive structures. The widely known conservation tasks provide an example: a child concludes that the quantity of beans poured from a wide jar to a narrow jar remains constant, while questioning whether or not the quantity of water poured from jar to jar remains constant (Piaget and Szeminska 1965). While both are conservation tasks (the group of individual beans represent discontinuous quantity and the water represents continuous quantity), the child conserves in one domain and not the other. This is known as décalage. Décalage refers to the gap between an individual's use of a cognitive structure in one domain and lack of immediate transfer of that structure to other domains.

In another example, a child states that water poured from one jar to another jar of a different shape is unchanged, while questioning whether or not coffee beans weigh the same before and after grinding (Sigel and Cocking 1977). Again, both are conservation tasks, but the child thinks about conservation using different mental structures when the content (continuous or discontinuous quantity) is different. Thus, our understandings of the notion of décalage caution us against using broad labels with students.[1]

Constructivist teachers design lessons that address students' suppositions. This design process is informed and enhanced by an understanding of the cognitive demands implied by certain curricular tasks. For example, a lesson on the manipulation of fractions can invite students into a confrontation with their previous constructions of part-whole relationships. Similarly, lessons asking students to consider reasons that both the allied and axis nations engaged in World War II can help students consider multiple frames of reference. The adaptation of curricular tasks to address student suppositions is a function of the cognitive demands implicit in specific tasks (the curriculum) and the nature of the questions posed by the students engaged in these tasks (the suppositions). Bruner (1971) uses the term "mismatch" to refer to the delicate relationship between a student's questions, which are reflective of current mental structures, and the ideas within immediate reach:

> The teacher needs to have procedures for determining "appropriate mismatches" and the extent to which the child's learning is dependent on figurative and/or operative processes (p. 67).

The pertinent message here for educators is that we don't know what ideas are within students' reach unless we do something specific to find out. That is why our first three foundational principles—posing problems of emerging relevance (Chapter 4), structuring learning around primary concepts (Chapter 5), and seeking and valuing students' points of view (Chapter 6)—are so important. They are practices that guide teachers in adapting curricular demands to students' suppositions.

---

[1]Readers wanting a more detailed discussion of cognitive developmental theory can refer to Piaget's groundbreaking works (1952, 1967, 1974, 1987), the many excellent books that describe Piaget's conceptualizations of mental structures and his carefully articulated clinical tasks (Ginsburg and Opper 1969; Wadsworth 1971, 1978; Cowan 1978; Labinowicz 1980, 1985), and some of the critiques citing the limitations of Piaget's theories (Haroutunian 1983, Gardner 1991b, Case 1985, 1991). See the bibliography of this book.

The following five classroom examples illustrate how teachers think about curriculum adaptation and analyze classroom events.

1st Graders Study Math

During a 1st grade math lesson on measurement and equivalency, children were asked to use a balance to determine how many plastic links equaled one metal washer in weight. The teacher recognized and seized an opportunity to help one particularly eager child, Anna, begin to construct a rudimentary notion of ratio and proportion.

Teacher: How many links does it take to balance one washer?

Anna: (After a few seconds of experimenting) Four.

Teacher: If I placed one more washer on this side, how many more links do you think we would need to balance it?

Anna: One.

Teacher: Try it.

Anna placed one more link in the balance tray and noticed that balance was not achieved. She looked confused and placed another link in the tray and then a third. Still no balance. She placed one more link in the tray. Balance was achieved. She smiled and looked at the teacher.

Teacher: How many cubes did it take to balance one washer?

Anna: Four.

Teacher: And how many to balance two washers?

Anna: (counting) Eight.

Teacher: If I put one more washer on this side, how many more links will you need to balance it?

Anna: (Pondered and looked quizzically at the teacher) Four.

Teacher: Try it.

Anna: (after successfully balancing with four links) Each washer is the same as four links.

Teacher: Now, let me give you a really hard question. If I took Four links off of the balance, how many washers would I need to take off in order to balance it?

Anna: One!

When, how, and upon which content a teacher asks students to engage in such activities is a dynamic decision made by the teacher, and informed by an understanding of the student's suppositions. Each answer a student offers to a teacher's questions reveals suppositions the student is making about the issue at hand. Knowing the student's suppositions enables the teacher to adapt the curriculum to address them. For example, another child in this class, Melissa, indicated that three, not four, plastic links equalled one washer. The teacher's first response was "Try again," but when he approached Melissa's desk and asked her to show him how she got three, Melissa happily took the washer out of the balance, placed it on her desk, and surrounded it with three chain links in a triangular shape (see Figure 7.1).

FIGURE 7.1

Melissa was not attempting to find equivalency in terms of weight. Rather, the spatial arrangement was salient in her mind, and she answered correctly the question she was asking herself. Without using geometric terms, she tried to equate the circumference of the outside circle of the washer and the inside shape created by the ring of links. Pursuing elaboration of her notion of circumference or re-directing the child's focus to weight or other types of teacher mediation that validated Melissa's current ideas and used them to help her segue her thoughts into other domains are all examples of adapting the cognitive demands of the curriculum to address a student's suppositions.

In this case, the teacher rethought his initial response "Try again," and chose to help Melissa move from equality in the spatial realm to equality of weight. He asked Melissa to place a chain link in one hand and a washer in the other.

"Which one is heavier?" he asked. Melissa replied that the washer felt heavier. The teacher then asked Melissa to try to figure out how many chain links weighed about the same as one washer, using her hands. Though the lesson ended shortly because the students moved to music class, the teacher ended with a beginning, knowing how he was going to work with Melissa at the next opportunity. He would continue to help her make the transition from space to weight.

Originally, the teacher was seeking only the "right" answer. Lost in this search was the richness of Melissa's perspective . . . until the teacher sought it. The beauty of multiple perspectives and the energy of creative thought are often lost in classrooms. Students in classrooms that emphasize "rightness" and "wrongness" cease to offer their views on issues unless they feel confident that their views are shared by the teacher. In effect, only one perspective gets acknowledged and discussed, and the classroom becomes an acutely parochial setting.

2nd Graders Study Science

In the 1st grade example, the teacher adapted the lesson because at least one student brought to the task a supposition quite divergent from the one addressed by the curriculum guide. Two 2nd grade teachers learned the importance of constantly monitoring student understanding and adapting lessons accordingly when their 44 students completed a task in a surprising way. In these two 2nd grade classrooms, students were studying "Changes in Fall." The teachers encouraged the students to consider the topic through questions such as: What makes a tree in the fall look differently? Are all leaves the same? Are all trees the same color? What does a leaf look like? Can I describe some changes I observe? Do I see patterns?

After seeing filmstrips, taking a nature walk, collecting leaves, making leaf rubbings, observing trees around the school, and drawing, laminating, and classifying fall leaves, the teachers felt that the experience had been "concretized" sufficiently to allow the children to generalize to similar situations. Yet, when asked to "paint a fall picture," and given a full range of paints, every child in the class painted green trees.

The teachers concluded that the activities in which the students had just engaged had not influenced their conceptions of how one paints a picture of a fall tree. They realized that for these 2nd graders, looking at individual leaves and looking at a whole tree generated separate understandings. This led the teachers to think about how teachers really know what their students learn from various lessons? They were reminded that, in their words, "teachers must constantly question the children as to what they are doing and observing . . . dialogue must constantly occur" (Jehle and Reynolds 1983).

These first two examples illustrate the necessity to provide both precursor and extension activities to lessons suggested by the curriculum publisher or designed by the teacher.

6th Graders Study Social Studies

Another example of how learning opportunities are enhanced by differentiated curriculum experiences involves *Man: A Course of Study* (MACOS), an interdisciplinary curriculum designed for 10-year-old students by Jerome Bruner and his colleagues in the 1960s and still used today in some schools. In one 6th grade class, students using MACOS explored the biology and lifecycle of the salmon. The students were asked to think about experiments designed and implemented by scientists who study the habits and behavior of salmon. The students were presented with data revealing that almost all salmon return to their homestreams, but that only one-quarter of salmon with plugged nostrils return to their homestreams. They were then asked questions such as: "What innate ability of salmon helps them find their homestreams?"

One approach to answering this question requires proportional and correlational reasoning. Correlational reasoning is the ability to conclude that there is or is not a relationship, whether negative or positive, between two or more sets of data. Students studying the salmon can distinguish between and compare the ratio of fish whose natural olfactory sense had been affected with the ratio of those fish whose sense had not. Very few of the students, however, were then able to compare the differential ratios to data about whether or not the fish arrived back at their homestreams. But some of the students were able to generate correlations with teacher mediation.

The teacher asked the students to describe their thinking. She realized that they had trouble keeping their "if . . . then " statements clear. The teacher viewed their grappling with the language as their way of coming to understand the concept. For these students, the teacher provided curriculum that addressed their suppositions as revealed by the questions they were ready to pose. However, for the majority of students in the class, no correlations could be deduced. Their suppositions about fish behavior and sensory deprivation did not allow them to generate much new knowledge from the "scientific" data presented.

The teacher had to adapt the curriculum to maximize the likelihood that it would facilitate the development of correlational reasoning, or the precursors to it, or help students generate some new knowledge of fish behavior. She did this simply by reflecting questions back to students. One student asked how the scientist plugged the salmon's nostrils. The teacher reflected the question back to the class, then orchestrated student-to-student dialogues. Subsequent questions and hypotheses began to fly: Did they use poles or nets? Why didn't the fish die while they were out of the water? How long can fish stay out of the water? How could they breathe if their nostrils were plugged? Do fish breathe through their nostrils? Blank stares turned to directed gazes and understandings began to emerge. The teacher stayed within the general concept, adapted her lesson plans, and fostered the emerging relevance of the concept for her students. Once some relevance was established, the students engaged in the curriculum with the commitment that fosters understanding.

7th Graders Study English/Social Studies

Let's continue our discussion of adapting curriculum to address students' suppositions by looking at a 7th grade English/social studies class beginning a unit on Greek mythology. Much literature in the field of cognitive development states that students need a rich repertoire of experiences and actions (Arlin 1975) in order to develop abstract thought structures in specific content areas. This doesn't mean that students must necessarily have repertoires of experiences and actions relating directly to the topic

77

being studied (in this case, Greek mythology), but rather to the large concepts that underlie the topic. In keeping with this premise, tasks within this Greek myth unit required 7th graders to seriate events, classify character behavior, and conserve character intentions even when behaviors changed. These structures are precursors to the structures of induction and propositional logic, abilities that these 12- and 13-year-old students were just developing.

The first activity involved sequencing. The teacher invited students to reveal their understandings of the Hera myth through discussion of main events and the transformation of those events into simple sentences the groups shared in flowcharts of varying designs. Students were encouraged to embellish the flowcharts with illustrations of the events. Some groups designated a specific color for each character, as well as specific designs to indicate the characters' emotions.

The following flowchart was created by one group of students:

FIGURE 7.2

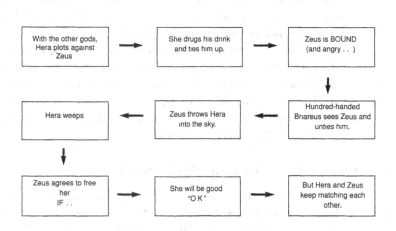

The next assignment invited the students to consider beginning notions of hypothetical reasoning. This activity was inspired by Edward Packard's series, *Design Your Own Adventure*. Packard sequences his plots through logical possibilities. His initial setting can yield as many as 30 or 40 storylines by having readers choose from various alternatives at critical times. For instance, in one series, the main character enters a western town. The reader must decide whether he should go to the sheriff, to the hotel, or to the newspaper office. For each choice, Packard develops a different sequence of events that fits logically with subsequent sets of choices.

After having read several Packard books to each other in class, the students asked if they could try to write their own stories. The teacher had planned to use the Packard stories as models for the students to follow in describing the Hera myth. But, their enthusiasm for the hypothetical premise of the books was so strong, she changed her original focus.

Some groups chose to create new stories and characters other than the gods, some chose the Greek gods. Here is one groups' response:

FIGURE 7.3

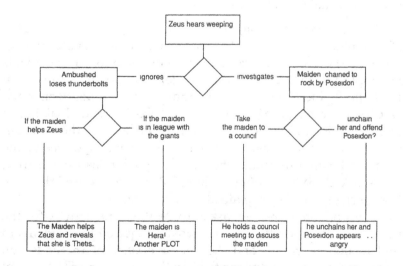

Few students had problems with the format, although some struggled with the imaginative demands of the task. The students eventually produced 16- to 20-page books on colored construction paper, illustrated with pictures, and bound with designed covers. Students were eager to read one another's stories and although the teacher had spent all year coaching them on nonjudgmental feedback, they commented to each other in decidedly evaluative tones, gen- erally positive.

During this lesson, students who were able to reason hypothetically were encouraged to do so. For the majority of the students, who didn't exhibit evidence of this type of reasoning, guidance was provided by the teacher when requested. For some groups, the teacher reduced the complexity of the hypothetical portion of the task by having an established pattern that students could follow. She even presented to some groups a blank flowchart model, although she worried that she might be robbing them of the opportunity to create something themselves for the purpose of expediting the final product. What surprised her was the students' eagerness to receive the help. Showing some students an example of a "final" product before they struggled too long made their goal a more attainable reality, rather than an overwhelming task they couldn't visualize completing.

In a subsequent lesson, the students were presented with 25 to 30 different common household objects, including a battery, a pot holder, a shoelace, and a container of suntan lotion. The students were asked to generate as many categories as possible utilizing at least three objects per category. Some of the student-generated categories were: games, red objects, plastic, medicinal items, kitchen tools, and square objects. By coincidence, the assistant principal entered the room during this lesson and, upon seeing the students busily examining the odd array of items on the front desks, asked, "What's going on here?" The students used the term "categorizing" as they explained their assignment.

The students were then asked to do the same activity for the Greek gods and goddesses. This activity required the students to understand the myths and the characteristics of the gods and goddesses sufficiently enough to align them in categories. Some of the categories the students devised were: gods and goddesses without children, children of Zeus, gods whose names begin with the letter H, and gods and goddesses who had temples built for them.

The introduction of this task involved the cognitive structure called classification. Students were asked to spontaneously generate the classification categories and apply those categories to the list of items. Judging the characteristics of gods and goddesses, based mostly or solely on reading material, is an abstract process through which students were asked to reason inductively. Although the framework of the task was classificatory, the teacher made the framework more accessible to the students through the use of common materials. Such activities challenge students. The element of novelty attracts them, yet the security of their being able to use an intact cognitive structure gives them a sense of confidence.

8th Graders Study Science

Let's examine Katie's experience with a "Weights and Pulleys" unit in her 8th grade science class. The introductory lesson called for giving the students single- and double-wheeled pulleys, weights, and string and asking them to "play" in pairs. During this time, while other students eagerly created simple machines, Katie talked with her partner.

The second lesson began with a worksheet explaining sequential steps, a chart on which students were to keep notes, and considerable teacher direction for weighing various objects and testing "force to type of pulley" relationships. Katie made only the first machine. She could weigh the object with a spring scale, but could not understand how to discover force.

As part of the third lesson, the students were asked to consider two pictures, one of a single pulley with a 100 lbs. bucket serving as a weight and one of a more complex pulley system with a 100 lbs. block serving as a weight. The teacher used this opportunity to ascertain the nature of Katie's understanding of the concepts explored up to this point. The teacher asked Katie, "In which picture do you think it would be easier to lift the object?"

Katie chose the complex pulley. The teacher asked why. Katie responded that the bucket was heavier. Although she chose the picture her teacher suspected she would, the teacher couldn't understand her reasoning. The teacher, unsure that Katie comprehended that the weight in each system was the same, drew the label "100 lbs." on each picture. The following dialogue ensued:

Teacher: They each weigh 100 lbs. Do they weigh the same?
Katie: Yes.
Teacher: Which one is heavier?
Katie: The bucket.
Teacher: Why?
Katie: Because the bucket's heavier.
Teacher: But they each weigh 100 lbs.
Katie: But the bucket has sand in it and it looks heavier.

At this point, it became clear to the teacher that a lesson designed to help foster an understanding of the mechanical advantage of various pulley systems was inappropriate for Katie because her reasoning with regard to these tasks appeared to be perception-bound. The teacher concluded that the opportunity for Katie to weigh with some peers a number of objects varying in density and relative size would encourage her to formulate a definition of weight and would offer her greater opportunities for growth than did the pulley assignment.

The Role of Errors in Cognitive Development

Cognitive developmental literature identifies certain behaviors associated with various egocentric states in children (Copple et. al 1984, Labinowicz 1980). The perceptual boundedness of the preschool child and the lack of differentiation between fact and assumption seen in the elementary school child (Elkind 1974) have observable behavioral correlates. The child effectively mediates experiences through the observation of his own actions and moves the behavior to another plane, that of thought. Reflective abstraction (Ginsburg and Opper 1979) is the child's consideration of his own actions as the means for learning to occur.

In the classroom, the operant expression of the child's abstractions may appear to be "incorrect" if one uses adult logic as the criterion by which "correctness" is judged. Dewey (1902) wrote:

> The fundamental factors in the educative process are an immature, undeveloped being, and certain social aims, meanings, and values incarnate in the matured experience of the adult (p. 4).

Therefore, it's important not to impose adult expectations on a child's thought processes, but, rather, to look at the child's behavior as a manifestation of movement to an ensuing way of reasoning. "A child's errors are actually natural steps to understanding" (Labinowicz 1980). The ability to listen effectively and gather information regarding cognitive and affective functioning and the subsequent ability to adapt teaching methodologies are the heart of what we, as educators, can provide for students.

Adapting curriculum doesn't necessarily imply editing out certain curricular materials or changing the order of the materials' presentation. Nor does it necessarily imply that material well-matched to the child's present suppositions will automatically be learned. The process is not so simple. Teacher mediation is a key factor in this complex equation. The teacher can obstruct student learning or help students build their own bridges from present understandings to new, more complex understandings. Although it's the teacher who structures the opportunity, it's the students' own reflective abstractions that create the new understanding.

Dewey (1902), in discussing the importance of seeking to uncover the student's perceptions and interests wrote:

> Selected, utilized, emphasized, [activities of interest to students] may mark a turning point for good in the child's whole career; neglected, an opportunity goes, never to be recalled (p. 14).

References

Arlin, P.K. (1975). "Cognitive Development in Adulthood: A Fifth Stage?" *Developmental Psychology* 11, 5: 602-606.

Bruner, J., (1971). *The Relevance of Education*. N.Y.: Norton.

Copple, C., I Sigel, and R. Saunders. (1984). *Educating the Young Thinker.* New York: D. Van Nostrand.

Cowan, P. (1978). *Piaget: With Feeling*. N.Y.: Holt, Rinehart and Winston.

Dewey, J. (1902). *The Child and the Curriculum*. Chicago: University of Chicago Press.

Elkind, D. (1970). *Children and Adolescents: Interpretive Essays on Jean Piaget*. New York: Oxford University Press.

Elkind, D. (1974). *A Sympathetic Understanding of the Child, Birth to Sixteen*. Boston: Allyn and Bacon, Inc.

Elkind, D. (1976). *Child Development and Education: A Piagetian Perspective*. New York: Oxford University Press.

Erikson, E.H. (1950). *Childhood and Society*. New York: Norton.

Gilligan, C. (1982). *In a Different Voice*. Cambridge, Mass.: Harvard University Press.

Ginsburg, H., and S. Opper. (1979). *Piaget's Theory of Intellectual Development: An Introduction*. Englewood Cliffs, N.J.: Prentice Hall.

Haroutunian, S. (1983). *Equilibrium in the Balance*. New York: Springer-Verlag.

Inhelder, B., H. Sinclair, and M. Bovet. (1974). *Learning and the Development of Cognition*. Cambridge, Mass.: Harvard University Press.

Jehle, H., and C. Reynolds. (1983). Unpublished manuscript. New York: Shoreham-Wading River Schools.

Kohlberg, L. (1969). *Stages in the Development of Moral Thought and Action*. New York: Holt, Rinehart & Winston.

Labinowicz, E. (1985). *Learning from Children: New Beginnings for Teaching Numerical Thinking*. Menlo Park, Calif.: Addison-Wesley.

Labinowicz, E. (1980). *The Piaget Primer: Thinking, Learning, Teaching*. Menlo Park, Calif: Addison Wesley.

Lowery, L. (1974a). *Learning About Instruction: Questioning*. Berkeley: University of California.

Lowery, L. (1974b). *Learning About Learning: Classification Abilities*. Berkeley: University of California.

Lowery, L. (1974b). *Learning About Learning: Conservation Abilities*. Berkeley: University of California.

Piaget, J., and C. Szeminska. (1965). *The Child's Conception of Number*. New York: Norton.

Sigel, I.E., and R.R. Cocking. (1977). *Cognitive Development from Childhood to Adolescence: A Constructivist Perspective*. N.Y.: Holt, Rinehart and Winston.

Wadsworth, B. (1978). *Piaget for the Classroom Teacher*. New York: Longman.

8

Principle #5

Assessing Student Learning in the Context of Teaching

W
e have all been in classrooms where the teacher poses a question to the students and hands shoot up excitedly. The teacher then peers about the room and calls on a student. The student answers, and the teacher says, "No." The teacher then calls on a second student. That student answers, and the teacher, shaking his head from side to side, says, "Uh-uh." The teacher then calls upon a third student, and as she answers, the teacher says, "Close, but not quite." A fourth intrepid student raises his hand. Upon answering, the teacher shakes his head affirmatively and says, "Yes, THAT'S the right answer!"

What implicit lessons do such teacher behaviors convey to students? Probably several. First, students learn that there is one correct answer to each question posed by the teacher, and that their challenge is to come up with that answer. Second, they learn that they place themselves at some risk if they raise their hands before being certain that they have figured out the one, right answer. The teacher is not apt to say, "Gee, I never thought about it that way. Can you say more about that?" or "That's a creative way of looking at the issue. How did you arrive at that answer?" Instead, the teacher's likely response is "No" unless the student offers the precise answer being sought.

The problem with such lessons is clear. "No" hurts and makes students feel invalidated and foolish. "No" communicates to students that their idiosyncratic thinking about issues is not particularly valued. It erodes their desire to think about and explore issues, which leads them to be preoccupied instead by the far less valuable activity of predicting the answer the teacher wants.

Students pay a price in such situations, and so do teachers. Posing narrow questions for which one seeks a singular answer denies teachers the opportunity to peer into students' minds. Creativity and risk taking are not attributes that can be turned on and off. Both need nurturing, encouragement, and support. Creative thinking is not something that can be scheduled during a particular segment of the school day, separated from the rest of the academic program. There is widespread belief that the study of math and science seeks right answers, while the study of literature and the humanities accepts creativity. Students who learn in settings that encourage individual construction of knowledge do not see the content area boundaries so clearly. Learning about our world is inherently interdisciplinary. Solving our world's problems requires creative thought. The big price paid by teachers who emphasize "rightness" is losing the ability to evoke creative student work. Bruner (1971) writes:

> It is my hunch that it is only through the exercise of problem solving and the effort of discovery that one learns the working heuristics of discovery; the more one has practice, the more likely one is to generalize what has been learned into a style of problem solving or inquiry that serves for any kind of task encountered—or almost any kind of task. Of only one thing am I convinced: I have never seen anybody improve in the art and technique of inquiry by any means other than engaging in inquiry (p. 94).

Bruner's hunch is consistent with Piaget's foundational theory and the operating premise of constructivist teaching. Real inquiry is inherently interdisciplinary, and interdisciplinary problems are inherently broad and open ended. Such problems rarely have one, easily accessible right answer.

Rightness and Wrongness

What exactly are right and wrong answers? To the question, "Can you name one of the three ships involved in Columbus' voyage to the Indies?" "Pinta" is right and "Merrimac" is wrong. This seems reasonably straightforward, but it is actually quite complex.

Students often correctly hear the questions posed by teachers, but they simply don't know the answers. It is also true that students often correctly answer the questions they ask themselves—the questions they *think* they hear their teachers ask. It would be interesting to know what question the student thought he was answering when stating "Merrimac." If the student was answering a different question from the one the teacher posed, knowing that question would help the teacher to re-orient the student to the explorer at hand and to assess the student's present understanding of the time period. If the student understood the question in the same manner the teacher had in mind, the teacher would know (1) that the student hadn't yet assimilated certain specific information, and (2) that "Merrimac" means *something* to the student and could be a window into the student's point of view.

"Rightness" and "wrongness," then, relate as much to the filtering system used by adults to sort through students' responses as to the students' conceptions of the issues and questions to which they respond. To teachers, inaccurate responses are "wrong." To students, inaccurate responses often represent the state of their current thinking about topics.

Think of how different the learning and assessment processes in school would be if teachers came to view themselves as cognitively linked with the students they teach. Rather than using assessment results as indices only of individual student knowledge, such information might shed light on the relationship between the student and the teacher. In this paradigm, the student is not assessed in isolation, but in conjunction with the teacher, and both learn as a result of assessment. Newman, Griffin, and Cole (1989) speak to this point:

> Instead of giving the children a task and measuring how well they do or how badly they fail, one can give the children the task and observe how much and what kind of help they need in order to complete the task successfully. In this approach the child is not assessed alone. Rather, the social system of the teacher and child is dynamically assessed to determine how far along it has progressed (pp. 77-78).

In this approach, the teacher is able to monitor simultaneously the cognitive functioning of the student, the disposition of the student, and the status of the teacher/student relationship. Student conceptions, rather than indicating "rightness" or "wrongness," become entry points for the teacher, places to begin the sorts of intervention that lead to the learner's construction of new understandings and the acquisition of new skills.

How does the teacher offer intervention of that nature? By using assessment as a tool in service to the learner, rather than as an accountability device and not as a teacher effectiveness measure, teachers can begin to rethink the dynamic relationship between teaching and assessment. Let's get to know 12-year-old Greg, and see if that acquaintance clarifies the connection between teaching and assessment.

Assessment in Service to the Learner: A Case Study

Greg is a 7th grader in a child-centered middle school. He achieves minimal academic success and demonstrates a noticeably subdued affect. He just isn't "making it" in school. Throughout his academic folder, there are teacher comments such as: "Greg has failed to complete five assignments and has not accepted offers of extra help." Due to limited academic success, Greg has been put in remedial math and English classes since the primary grades. Affectively, he evidences lethargy, apathy, and isolation. He chooses seats peripheral to the other students and teacher, frequently comments on being tired, and oversleeps many mornings. Prior medical examinations have revealed no physical ailments.

Greg's apparent indifference is especially evident in his Spanish class. Seeking a way of reaching him, the teacher decided to focus more of her attentions on Greg in order to determine specifically the types of problem-solving skills he demonstrates in the context of language translation.

On one particular morning, another student was presenting a report describing his term project, a study of the international, little-spoken language, Esperanto. The student gave his peers one paragraph in English and a second one translated into Esperanto

FIGURE 8.1

A professor of zoology did not like it very much when his students entered late at the beginning of his lecture, and at that time, interrupting his reading, he always expressed his annoyance to the tardy students. On one occasion, when the professor was reading about a horse, a certain tardy student entered the classroom. To the amazement of the students, contrary to his custom, the professor said nothing to the student and continued his reading. Finishing his reading about the horse, he said, "Now, gentlemen, after the horse let us turn to the donkey," and turning toward the latecomer, he said, "I beg you sit down." "Do not get excited, Mr. Professor," replied the student. "I can listen to a donkey standing, too."

Profesoro de zoologio tre ne amis, kiam la studentoj malfruis al la komenco de la lekcio kaj tiam, interrompante sian legadon, li ciam esprimadis sian malplezuron al la malfruinta studento. Un fojon, kiam la profesoro legis pri cevalo, eniris en la legejon iu malfruinta studento. Al la miro de la studentoj, kontrau sia kutimo la profesoro nenion diris al la studento kaj daurigis sian legadon. Fininte la legadon pri cevalo, li diris: — Nun, sinjoroj, post la "cevalo" ni transiru al la "azeno," kaj, turninte sin al la malfruinta, li diris: Mi petas, sidigu. — Ne maltrankviligu vin, sinjoro profesoro, respondis la studento, mi povas auskulti azenon ankau starante.

and asked the class to select the Esperanto equivalent for 10 English words (see figure 8.1).

Greg attempted to find the Esperanto word by matching the line on which the English word appeared with the line on which the Esperanto word appeared. But just as Piaget and Szeminska (1965, p. 143) found that infants who employed a new strategy and did not meet with immediate success reverted to earlier, more primitive strategies, so did Greg forsake his new strategies when they were not immediately successful. When Greg's first attempt at translation proved unsuccessful, he put down his pencil and said: "I don't know how to do this." The following dialogue ensued:

Teacher: The way that you tried didn't work. What can you do now?

Greg: I don't know.

Teacher: You started out counting. Can you change it somehow to make it work?

Greg: No.

Teacher: You first counted the lines. I wonder if it would work out to count the sentences?

Greg: Oh, yeah. (lifting his body closer to the table)

Greg successfully used the sentence counting technique and modified it as he worked. To find a word at the end of the paragraph, he said: "I know, I'll do it backwards. It's the 2nd to the last sentence."

On longer sentences, he identified a criterion relating to the position of the English words relative to the commas.

When the Esperanto equivalent was a phrase, and thus not a word-to-word match, Greg reverted to stating "I don't know" after two or three attempts to isolate the one word for which he was looking. The following dialogue shows his readiness to employ and understand further strategies that were originally hidden by his initially indifferent responses.

Teacher: Now we have a whole sentence. This one is tougher What do you think the answer is?

Greg: I don't know.

Teacher: How many words are there in the English sentence?

Greg: (Counting) Eight.
(He then immediately begins to count the words in the Esperanto sentence.)
Six. Some of them can be together like "sit down." (referring to a previous item.)

Teacher: I think you're onto something. Keep going.

Greg continued to make inferences based on criteria other than sentence position alone. He suggested that "standing, too" could be re-worded as "also standing." Therefore, the Esperanto word beginning with "st" could mean "standing," although it was the last word in the Esperanto sentence. Greg continued to apply and infer certain syntactical and grammatical rules once the teacher acknowledged that he was "onto something." His teacher reasoned that Greg perceives himself as wasting time, and as allowing himself to be hurt, when he perseveres on assignments that are returned to him highly corrected. Because Greg's concepts about himself, like other conceptualizations, are influenced by the feedback he receives from others, his lack of progress in Spanish class seems to have more to do with his graphic skills (unconventional spelling and cryptic sentences), coupled with low self-esteem, than an inability to successfully reason out the translation process.

In this example, Greg wasn't initially willing to take risks when confronted with problems for which he had no immediate solution. However, when he was offered ways of modifying his own strategies, he appeared more willing to take risks and reveal his thought processes. Even in a child-centered school that explicitly values intellectual autonomy, Greg has been in a number of classrooms with many "right" answers, and he hasn't often known many of those answers. Greg's Spanish teacher doubts that he takes his own thinking very seriously. Indeed, when periodically given feedback focused on the particular task at hand, Greg often chooses not to engage himself in the dialogue.

Many factors are involved in Greg's functioning, several of which may be far beyond that which the school can affect. However, when Greg was presented with nonjudgmental feedback that implicitly valued his ideas and comments, he appeared willing to take risks and engage in the task. It's important to note here that, in the process of assessing Greg's understanding of language constructs, the teacher was also able to help Greg to learn about some of those same constructs. Assessment and teaching merged in service to the learner.

Nonjudgmental Feedback

Let's consider the difficulties in providing nonjudgmental feedback by looking at a university preservice teacher education class. The class was divided into groups, given a problem to solve, and then asked to write up and post their approaches and conclusions. Each group had to then respond to other groups' work and provide feedback of a nature that would invite further work by the group. The problem was taken from the Vermont Assessment Program (Vermont Department of Education 1991):

Cars and Trees

A mature tree can utilize 13 lbs. of carbon dioxide a year. The average car spews out 4000 lbs. of CO_2 per year. How many mature trees would you need to utilize this much CO_2? There are approximately 183 million cars in the United States. Using these data, how many trees would be needed to utilize all the CO_2 spewed out by all the cars in the United States each year?

Carbon dioxide emissions are directly related to car efficiency. Doubling the fuel efficiency roughly halves CO_2 emissions. The average car on the road averages 18 miles per gallon. At this efficiency rating a car emits approximately 58 tons of CO_2 in its lifetime.

Make a line graph that shows what happens as the fuel efficiency is doubled. Then, use the graph to determine the amount of CO_2 emitted at efficiency ratings of: 30 mpg; 35 mpg; 40 mpg; 50 mpg; and 60 mpg.

Below is a journal entry illustrating the challenge in offering nonjudgmental feedback. This entry was written by a preservice teacher, but it represents the same sentiments offered to us by teachers at various experience levels.

The first thing that I noticed was the difficulty in finding descriptions that were non-evaluative. "Good" was just as forbidden as "bad." I looked up "evaluate" in the dictionary. The definition was: to determine or fix the value of; to determine the significance or worth of. To determine the significance or worth of! How does a teacher determine what is significant in another person's learning? Is anyone's ability to communicate "worth" less than anyone else's? However, even though I feel that I understand why evaluating a person's work is not really a valid means of assessing what they have learned, to actually write a non-evaluative assessment was very difficult.

My group tried. Writing the evaluation without denigrating the work was tough. We were torn between not wanting to hurt the feelings of the other group members and wanting to show them how "inferior" their work was next to ours (we knew our written reports were *so* much better). Much to our surprise, the other group found our reports to be pretty faulty. We were not clear on many points (I think the "collective unconscious" might have been somewhat responsible). They had just as hard a time understanding our conclusions, as we had with theirs. How did I feel? Mortified. Insulted. Embarrassed. Most of all—defensive. I wanted to prove how wrong they were and how right I was, when actually it wasn't a question of wrong or right—it was a question of clarity. We all understood what the assignment was. We all did the same basic thing and came to the same basic conclusions. Nobody was right or wrong. Yet we were all getting very defensive in explaining our work, and denigrative when talking about "their" work. It made me realize how damaging it could be to someone's self-esteem if you rated them based on your understanding and not theirs (Griffin 1992).

A second journal entry illustrates the link between what a teacher asks students to consider and how the teacher structures classroom interactions. This preservice physics teacher continued to reflect on the problem of excess CO_2 emissions as well as the challenge of nonjudgmental teacher/student interactions:

I just got home and realized I had game 5 of the World Series on the car radio while driving and I don't know what happened. Why? Because I was realizing that my selection of a quadratic fit to describe the relationship between exhaust emissions and fuel efficiency wasn't working. Me, the most avid baseball fan of all time, missing an inning of the World Series because I was preoccupied. Was I "engaged" or what?

It's funny because my "paper" from the activity came back with a question as to why I chose to use a quadratic. I did because I had determined three points on a graph and with three sets of coordinates the only non-linear expression I could fit was quadratic. I couldn't see why "they" couldn't appreciate this having seen it and having used a linear model themselves, which provided at more than one point negative emissions. Anyway, I realized as I left class that what was really needed was a dying exponential function (e.g., e^{-x})

similar to the expression used for radioactive decay or heat loss. So, in effect, I had modified my response twice, from linear to quadratic to exponential, but the "criticism" was justified since I did not rationalize the use of a quadratic. I only indicated why linear was not acceptable.

Anyway, the most difficult aspect of assessing the work of someone else is to find nonjudgmental descriptors. I found it relatively easy to pose questions, although even then it was necessary to compose the question in such a way as not to imply judgments. For example, "why don't you . . ." is not a good way to phrase a question because it implies that the other person should have been doing something else and was therefore wrong. You had mentioned a series of descriptors, which were rich in language. Outside of using questions, I really could not come up with neutral descriptors. Do you have examples?

While we tried to be non-critical in our remarks/questions on the papers we evaluated, we still received a "strong" reaction from the submitters. I have to take it that we still, on our comments/questions, implied too much judgment of "rightness" or "wrongness." It would seem this is a skill that will take more time and effort to develop. Actually, when I reflect on it, it makes sense when you consider the ritual that most teachers go through after each test. They more or less get surrounded by students bringing their tests up, looking for a few extra points, claiming they were wrongfully marked for various reasons (Ferrandino 1991).

Thinking about nonjudgmental feedback to students provokes a number of questions about many traditional school practices. Why do we give tests? Why do we give grades? Does doing such facilitate learning? Or does it create an external factor that diverts students' minds from the intellectual demands of "real" learning onto the emotional concerns of one's comparative rating in the class?

It's difficult to structure assessment around nonjudgmental feedback because we are all so acculturated to use evaluative words and expressions. "No," "good," "right," and "wrong" are just a few of the words used over and over in schools. Upon hearing these words, students either continue or alter their thinking, not because of some internal realization but because of an external prompt. Over time, this sort of feedback makes students teacher-dependent.

Ferrandino's journal entry (1991) asked for some examples of nonjudgmental feedback. Teachers seeking to offer nonjudgmental feedback might think about responding to students' questions with additional questions, to students' assertions with plausible contradictions, to students' requests for assistance with requests for explanations of their thinking to date, and to students' arguments with responses such as "I can see that this is important to you," or "That's something I haven't studied very much," or "You've convinced me," or "Your idea makes sense to me; what do your classmates think of it?" Such reactions place the responsibility on students for assessing the efficacy of their own efforts, and make pleasing the teacher far less important. Consider the following discussion about a writing sample between a 10th grade English teacher and a student:

Student: I know that the piece flows, but do you think that it reads well?

Teacher: Why do you think it flows?

Student: Well, I mean that it works for me. I feel good about what I wrote.

Teacher: Why? What about the story touches you?

Student: Uh, it was a, you know, a difficult time in my life and I was confused and, you know, hurt a lot. I think that the story says that, don't you?

Teacher: Well, I hear now that you were confused, but when I read this section I sensed that you were assured. You used strong words to describe your actions.

Student: Well, I felt that I was right and no one gave me the benefit of the doubt. Maybe I'll take out the part about being confused. I really was angry, not confused.

The teacher's skill at responding to requests for evaluative feedback with questions and possible contradictions helped the student to clarify in her own mind the true emotions she wanted to capture in her story. It is also useful to note that the student, in the absence of evaluative feedback from the teacher, assessed the piece of writing herself, and found it to be to her liking.

Authenticity and Context

Authentic assessment, like learning, occurs most naturally and lastingly when it is in a meaningful context and when it relates to authentic concerns and problems faced by students. Encouraging teachers to teach in a manner that fosters individual construction of knowledge and then requiring them to assess students in a traditional, test-oriented manner communicates mixed messages to teachers and students. In addressing this phenomenon, Mayer (1961) discusses

> the rush of tests and examinations and weekly quizzes, of workbooks and homework, of recitations and catechisms by which children everywhere—but especially in America—are made to prove that they have learned their lessons. If the child cannot give back on demand what he has been taught, it is assumed that he has not learned it (p. 87).

Because testing drives teaching, most teachers will eventually cease much of their teaching and prepare their students for the reality of having to pass a multiple-choice test. Bruner (1971) reinforces the dangers of this sort of approach to education:

> A method of instruction should have the objective of leading the child to discover for himself. Telling children and then testing them on what they have been told inevitably has the effect of producing bench-bound learners whose motivation for learning is likely to be extrinsic to the task—pleasing the teacher, getting into college, artificially maintaining self-esteem. The virtues of encouraging discovery are of two kinds. In the first place, the child will make what he learns his own, will fit his discovery into the interior world of cultures that he creates for himself. Equally important, discovery and the sense of confidence it provides is the proper reward for learning (pp. 123-124).

Tests, then, particularly multiple-choice tests, are structured to determine whether students know information related to a particular body of knowledge—usually a curriculum guide or syllabus. The focus is outward, not inward, on material, not personal constructions. Therefore, the overarching question asked by the test is "Do you know this material?" Authentic activities (tasks and problems already relevant or of emerging relevance to students) also relate to a particular body of knowledge, but rather than structuring assessment around specific bits of information, they invite students to exhibit what they have internalized and learned through application. The overarching question posed by such activities is "What do you know?" These two overarching questions are quite different.

This book illustrates assessment tasks that students and teachers have found meaningful. However, we do not refer to them as assessment tasks, but rather as problems, broad concepts, big ideas, learning tasks, and classroom lessons. The point is: Differentiating between teaching and assessment is both unnecessary and counterproductive. Assessment through teaching, through participating in student/teacher interactions, through observing student/student interactions, and through watching students work with ideas and materials tells us more about student learning than tests and externally developed assessment tasks.

Assessment through teaching is natural, but not particularly easy. Indeed, from the teacher's perspective, constructing authentic classroom activities and assessing student learning through them represents a more difficult challenge than administering a multiple-choice test. Most multiple-choice tests are readily accessible, come with templates, and are easy to administer and score. It's almost always easier to teach and test the curriculum than to mediate and assess learning. Meaningful tasks are more difficult to construct and require the mindful engagement of the assessor. But the advantages of meaningful, context-bound assessment are manifest. First, learning continues while assessment occurs. Working through complex problems requires students to apply a priori understandings to new situations and to construct newly modified understandings. In the traditional test-teach-test model, the process of learning all but shuts down while assessment occurs. Second, because authentic assessment tasks require students to apply prior knowledge to new situations, the teacher is able to distinguish between what students have memorized and what they have internalized. Third, context-bound assessment makes multiple paths to the same end equally valid. In discussing what they call "assessment while teaching," Newman, Griffin, and Cole (1989) note:

Many instructional units do not decompose themselves into a neat sequence of levels to be mastered in an invariant sequence with a single correct route to mastery. In fact, appropriable child behaviors come in great variety, requiring flexible expertise on the teacher's part to weave them into a productive instructional interaction (pp. 80).

A weaver, an explorer, an analyst . . . we have described the teacher in many ways. Now, let's look at the specific behaviors that comprise these diverse functions.

References

Bruner, J. (1971). *The Relevance of Education*. N.Y.: Norton.

Elkind, D. (Spring 1969). "Piagetian and Psychometric Conceptions of Intelligence." *Harvard Educational Review* 39, 2: 319-337.

Elkind, D. (1970). *Children and Adolescents: Interpretive Essays on Jean Piaget*. New York: Oxford University Press.

Elkind, D. (1976). *Child Development and Education: A Piagetian Perspective*. New York: Oxford University Press.

Ferrandino, F. (1991). Unpublished manuscript. New York: SUNY at Stony Brook.

Griffin, M. (October 24, 1992). Unpublished manuscript. New York: SUNY at Stony Brook.

Kant, E. (1965). *The Critique of Pure Reason*, trans. by N.K. Smith. New York: St. Martin's Press.

Kuhn, D., J. Langer, L. Kohlberg, and N.S. Haan. (1977). "The Development of Formal Operations in Logical and Moral Judgment." *Genetic Psychology Monographs* 95: 97-188.

Mayer, M. (1961). *The Schools*. New York: Doubleday and Company.

Newman, D., P. Griffin, and M. Cole. (1989). *The Construction Zone: Working for Cognitive Change in School*. Mass.: Cambridge University Press.

Piaget, J., and C. Szeminska. (1965). *The Child's Development from Childhood to Adolescence: A Constructivist Perspective*. N.Y.: Holt, Rinehart and Winston.

Sigel, I.E. (1978). "Constructivism and Teacher Education." *The Elementary School Journal* 78, 5.

Sigel, I.E. (May 1986). "Human Development and Teacher Education-or-What Teachers Are Not Taught About Human Development." Paper presented at the International Conference on Education, Chapel Hill, N.C.

Vermont Department of Education. (September 1991). *Vermont Mathematics Portfolio Project Teacher's Guide*. Burlington, Vt.: DOE.

PART III
Creating Constructivist Settings

Becoming a Constructivist Teacher

Pursuing Meaningful Victories

9

Becoming a Constructivist Teacher

Most teachers with whom we've met, regardless of the approaches they have used in the past, view constructivism as the way they've "always known people learn." Most of these teachers believe that they have been prevented from teaching in accord with that knowledge by a combination of rigid curriculums, unsupportive administrators, and inadequate preservice and inservice educational experiences. Once offered the opportunity to study and consider the role of constructivism in educational practice, they tend to view the inclusion of such teaching practices as natural and growth producing. Once teachers are exposed to these practices, they enthusiastically experiment with constructivist pedagogy until it becomes part of the very fabric of their classrooms.

Still, some teachers resist constructivist pedagogy. They usually do so for one of three reasons—commitment to their present instructional approach, concern about student learning, or concern about classroom control. Some teachers have told us that, although they are compelled by the power and promise of constructivist teaching, they are too deeply into their teaching careers to consider tearing down and rebuilding their instructional practices. Others see no reason to change because their current approaches seem to work well for their students; that is, their students take comprehensive notes and pass important tests; perform well on worksheets; complete assignments neatly and on time; write well-structured and well-researched individual or group reports; and receive good grades for their work. Still other teachers, while focused to varying degrees on how well they perceive their approaches have worked for students, are more concerned about how well their approaches have worked for them. These teachers tend to be more concerned with behavior management issues than with student learning, and they are fearful that the constructivist approach to teaching will erode some of their control. When a teacher arranges classroom dynamics so that she is the sole determiner of what is "right" in the classroom, most students learn to conform to expectations without critique, to refrain from questioning teacher directives, to seek permission from the teacher to move about the room, and to look to the teacher for judgmental and evaluative feedback. The rest disengage. Empowering students to construct their own understandings, therefore, is perceived by these teachers as a threatening break from the unwritten but widely understood hierarchical covenant that binds teachers and students.

Becoming a teacher who helps students to search rather than follow *is* challenging and, in many ways, frightening. Teachers who resist constructivist pedagogy do so for understandable reasons: most were not themselves educated in these settings nor trained to teach in these ways. The shift, therefore, seems enormous. And, if current instructional practices are perceived to be working, there is little incentive to experiment with new methodologies—even if the pedagogy undergirding the new methodologies is appealing.

But becoming a constructivist teacher is not as overwhelming as many teachers think. We have found that the following set of descriptors of constructivist teaching behaviors provides a useable framework within which teachers can experiment with this new approach. This set of descriptors presents teachers as mediators of students and environments, not simply as givers of information and managers of behavior. It is based on our own interactions with students and observations in the classrooms of many other teachers. The development of these descriptors has also been informed by the work of several researchers and theoreticians, including Sigel, Elkind, Kuhn, and Arlin (see bibliography).

1. Constructivist teachers encourage and accept student autonomy and initiative.

While the philosophies and mission statements of many schools purport to want students to be thinking, exploring individuals who generate hypotheses and test them out, the organizational and management structures of most schools militate against these goals. So, if autonomy, initiative, and leadership are to be nurtured, it must be done in individual classrooms.

Autonomy and initiative prompt students' pursuit of connections among ideas and concepts. Students who frame questions and issues and then go about answering and analyzing them take responsibility for their own learning and become problem solvers and, perhaps more important, problem finders. These students— in pursuit of new understandings—are led by their own ideas and informed by the ideas of others. These students ask for, if not demand, the freedom to play with ideas, explore issues, and encounter new information.

The way a teacher frames an assignment usually determines the degree to which students may be autonomous and display initiative. For example, students in a 12th grade English class read *Oedipus Rex*. The teacher asked the students to write an essay describing the book as Oliver Stone, the controversial film director, might think about it, and then to compare that interpretation to their understandings of Sophocles' views. To twig their interest, the teacher asked one group of students if they could find proof in the text that Oedipus had actually slept with his mother. After poring over the text, this group concluded that, according to the chronology of events, Oedipus could not possibly have done so. The students then wrote essays defending their positions and retold the story as they imagined Oliver Stone might have.

Conscientious students who are acculturated to receiving information passively and awaiting directions before acting will study and memorize what their teachers tell them is important. Robbing students of the opportunity to discern for themselves importance from trivia can evoke the conditions of a well-managed classroom at the expense of a transformation-seeking classroom.

2. Constructivist teachers use raw data and primary sources, along with manipulative, interactive, and physical materials.

Concepts, theorems, algorithms, laws, and guidelines are abstractions that the human mind generates through interaction with ideas. These abstractions emerge from the world of phenomena such as falling stars, nations at war, decomposing organic matter, gymnasts who can hurl their bodies through space, and all the other diverse happenings that describe our world. The constructivist approach to teaching presents these real-world possibilities to students, then helps the students generate the abstractions that bind these phenomena together. When teachers present to students the unusual and the commonplace and ask students to describe the difference, they encourage students to analyze, synthesize, and evaluate. Learning becomes the result of research related to real problems—and is this not what schools strive to engender in their students?

For example, students can read historical accounts of the effects of the social policies of the early 1980s on the economic and educational profile of the African-American population in the United States. Or, students can be taught to read the census reports and allowed to generate their own inferences about social policies. The former relies on the authority of a stranger. The latter relies on the ingenuity of the individual student. Lists of figures and pages of charts are probably not the first images evoked when the terms "hands on" or "manipulative" are heard. But the census data can tell a loud story if the right pages and lists are highlighted in the context of a good question.

3. When framing tasks, constructivist teachers use cognitive terminology such as "classify," "analyze," "predict," and "create."

The words we hear and use in our everyday lives affect our way of thinking and, ultimately, our actions. The teacher who asks students to select a story's main idea from a list of four possibilities on a multiple-choice test is presenting to the students a very different task than the teacher who asks students to analyze the relationships among three of the story's characters or predict how the story might have proceeded had certain events in the story not occurred. Analyzing, interpreting, predicting, and synthesizing are mental activities that require students to make connections, delve deeply into texts and contexts, and create new understandings.

In a 3rd grade classroom, a teacher read a story to her students about three children who became lost in a forest. After struggling mightily, yet unsuccessfully, to find their way, one of the three children, a brave and daring youngster, volunteers to go off alone in search of help while the other two wait in a clearing. At this point, the teacher stopped and asked the students to predict how the story is likely to end and to reveal the reasons behind their predictions: if a student predicts that help will be found and the other two children rescued, she is asked to indicate why. The overwhelming majority of students predicted just that—that all three would be rescued—and they explained their predictions by pointing to the competence of the child who went off in search of help. The students use information and impressions garnered from the text to predict how the story was likely to end. Framing tasks around cognitive activities such as analysis, interpretation, and prediction—and explicitly using those terms with students— fosters the construction of new understandings.

4. Constructivist teachers allow student responses to drive lessons, shift instructional strategies, and alter content.

This descriptor does *not* mean that students' initial interest, or lack of interest, in a topic determines whether the topic gets taught, nor does it mean that whole sections of the curriculum are to be jettisoned if students wish to discuss other issues. However, students' knowledge, experiences, and interests occasionally do coalesce around an urgent theme. Such was the case during the Persian Gulf War. Students at all grade levels were compelled by the images they saw, the reports they heard, and the fears they experienced. The social studies teacher attempting to continue discussions on the Renaissance, the science teacher moving ahead with the Krebs Cycle, and the art teacher in the middle of a unit on symmetry all experienced a similar phenomenon—the students were preoccupied with the war. When magnetic events occur that exert an irresistible pull on students' minds, continuing with pre-planned lessons is often fruitless.

This descriptor *does* address the notion of "teachable moments" throughout the school year. As educators, we have each experienced moments of excitement in the classroom, moments when the students' enthusiasm, interest, prior knowledge, and motivation have intersected in ways that made a particular lesson transcendental and enabled us to think with pride about that lesson for weeks. We recall the gleam in our students' eyes, their excitement about the tasks and discussions, and their extraordinary ability to attend to the task for long periods of time and with great commitment. If we were fortunate, we encountered a handful of these experiences each year, and wondered why they did not occur more frequently.

It's unfortunate that much of what we seek to teach our students is of little interest to them at that particular point in their lives. Curriculums and syllabi developed by publishers or state-level specialists are based on adult notions of what students of different ages need to know. Even when the topics are of interest to students, the recommended methodologies for teaching the topics sometimes are not. Little wonder, then, why more of those magnificent moments don't occur.

Although some teachers may not have much latitude regarding content, all generally have a good deal of autonomy in determining the ways in which the content is taught. For example, a certain elementary science curriculum called for students to begin learning about the "scientific method" and to conduct some rudimentary experiments using this method: ask a question (develop an hypothesis), figure out a way to answer the question (set up an experiment), tell what happens (record your observations), and answer the question (support or refute the initial hypothesis). One 5th grade teacher asked her students, in preparation for this assignment, to talk about their favorite things at home. One student, Jane, spoke about her cat. A classmate, Eric, discussed his house plants. Capitalizing on their responses, the teacher asked Jane and Eric to think of questions each had about the cat and the plants. Jane wanted to know if her cat would like other cat foods as much as he liked the brand he normally ate. Eric wanted to know how plants grow.

Through the teacher's mediation, Jane organized an experiment to answer her question about cat food. She arranged four different brands of cat food in four different bowls and placed them on the floor. When the cat entered the room, she observed which bowl he went to initially and from which bowl he ate. Jane changed the positions of the bowls and tried the experiment again. Ultimately, she concluded that her cat preferred one brand over the others.

With his teacher's mediation, Eric focused his question: Does the human voice affect the growth of a plant? Eric planted four bean seeds in four different pots and placed them all on the same shelf near a window. Each day he took each pot, one at a time, into another room. He spoke daily to one of the bean plants. He sang daily to a second plant. He yelled daily at a third plant. And he completely ignored the fourth. He recorded his observations over four weeks and concluded that the plants to which he spoke and sang grew the most.

The students' thinking drove these experiments, and the teacher's mediation framed the processes that followed. The curriculum content—exploration of the scientific method—was addressed faithfully in a different manner for each student.

5. Constructivist teachers inquire about students' understandings of concepts before sharing their own understandings of those concepts.

When teachers share their ideas and theories before students have an opportunity to develop their own, students' *questioning* of their own theories is essentially eliminated. Students assume that teachers know more than they do. Consequently, most students stop thinking about a concept or theory once they hear "the correct answer" from the teacher.

It's hard for many teachers to withhold their theories and ideas. First, teachers *do* often have a "correct answer" that they want to share with students. Second, students themselves are often impatient. Some students don't want to "waste their time" developing theories and exploring ideas if the teacher already knows that they are "on the wrong track." So teachers sometimes feel great pressure from students to offer the "right" answer. Third, some teachers adhere to the old saw about knowledge being power. Teachers struggling for control of their classes may use their knowledge as a behavior management device: when they share their ideas, the students are likely to be quiet and more attentive. And fourth, time is a serious consideration in many classrooms. The curriculum must be covered, and teachers' theories and ideas typically bring closure to discussions and move the class on to the next topic.

Constructivist teachers, the caveats presented in the preceding paragraph notwithstanding, withhold their notions and encourage students to develop their own thoughts. Approximated (or invented) spelling is a good example of this approach. As very young students are learning how to put words into writing, they begin to approximate the conventional spellings of words. A kindergarten student titled a sign language book she had illustrated by writing on the cover "My sin lnge bk." The teacher chose not to correct her spelling but, instead, to permit her to continue approximating the spelling of words. Interestingly, when reading the book at home to her parents only one day after writing this title, the girl said, "Oh, I left the two o's out of book." No one told the girl that her spelling was incorrect. She reformulated her own work in the process of sharing it. Her reformulation was a self-regulated event. The teacher's plan to share her understanding of the conventional spelling, in this case, became unnecessary.

6. Constructivist teachers encourage students to engage in dialogue, both with the teacher and with one another.

One very powerful way students come to change or reinforce conceptions is through social discourse. Having an opportunity to present one's own ideas, as well as being permitted to hear and reflect on the ideas of others, is an empowering experience. The benefit of discourse with others, particularly with peers, facilitates the meaning-making process.

Over the years, most students come to expect their teachers to differentiate between "good" and "bad" ideas, to indicate when responses are "right" and "wrong," and to transmit these messages in a fairly straightforward fashion. Dialogue is not a tile in the mosaic of school experienced by most students.

Consequently, most students learn to offer brief responses to questions, and to speak only when they are reasonably certain that they are supporting either a "good" idea or the "right" answer. These classroom sound bytes may assist teachers in moving speedily through the curriculum, but they don't help students construct new understandings or reflect on old ones.

A group of 8th grade teachers decided they wanted to offer a wider literature selection to their students and to engage the students in more thorough analyses of important ideas. They organized a series of Booktalks. In a Booktalk, a group of about eight students and an adult read and discuss the same book. The students select the book they wish to read from a master list compiled by the teachers, and the school's schedule is altered so that the groups can meet twice for 45 minutes during a three-week period. During the first meeting, the adult distributes the books to the students, sets the context for the book by asking questions about students' prior experiences that relate to the storyline, and begins to read the book aloud to the students. The second meeting is devoted to a discussion about the book.

In one Booktalk, students had read Steinbeck's *Of Mice and Men*. The issues raised by students during the post-reading discussion, issues generated by questions and contradictions posed by the teacher, included treatment of people with disabilities, sexism, the distribution of wealth and power in our nation, friendship, and death. The teacher orchestrated the discussion so that quiet students also had a chance to speak, but the ideas that drove the discussion belonged to the students and were fueled by student-to-student dialogue.

Student-to-student dialogue is the foundation upon which cooperative learning (Slavin 1990) is structured. Reports state that cooperative learning experiences have promoted interpersonal attraction among initially prejudiced peers (Cooper et al. 1980), and such experiences have promoted interethnic interaction in both instructional and free-time activities (Johnson et al. 1981).

The benefits of peer-to-peer dialogue among teachers reinforces its potential for students. Preservice teachers in one science methods course were asked to design, in cooperative learning groups, a system for a family to generate electricity for its home, using windmills. The stipulation that no batteries could be used was included in the instructions. During a whole-class discussion of each group's work-in-progress, the issue of energy storage led quickly to a discussion of batteries. Most students defined "battery" in terms of what one typically purchases in a store: an electrolytic cell such as the type used in toys and flashlights, or larger cells such as those used to power automobiles. Three students, however, demurred, and defined a battery as any device that can store energy, such as an expanded balloon or a tank of hot water. The dialogues that ensued resulted in, for some students, the transformation of perspectives and, for others, the onset of reflection on a new topic.

Two weeks later, while this same class grappled with another, seemingly simple problem—how to redraw silhouettes in half the original size—one student, after much consideration of the question, declared: "Now we're trying to figure out what 'half' really means. I still want to know: What is a battery!" In each of these sessions, the students addressed their questions and statements to one another. The teacher clarified the questions they raised of one another and demanded accuracy of word choice, but the communication currents were between and among the students and led to deeper understandings of the topics at hand.

7. Constructivist teachers encourage student inquiry by asking thoughtful, open-ended questions and encouraging students to ask questions of each other.

If we want students to value inquiry, we, as educators, must also value it. If teachers pose questions with the orientation that there is only one correct response, how can students be expected to develop either the interest in or the analytic skills necessary for more diverse modes of inquiry? Schools too often present students with one perspective: Columbus was a courageous explorer who discovered America (What does that imply about the Native Americans here when he came ashore?); and $Pi = 3.14$ (But C/d—circumference/diameter—yields another number; and if Pi is computed as the quotient of two integers, how can it be considered irrational?).

Complex, thoughtful questions challenge students to look beyond the apparent, to delve into issues deeply and broadly, and to form their own understandings of events and phenomena. Knowing, for example, that Columbus' ships carried with them diseases for which Native Americans had no antibodies and that Columbus and his men enslaved Native Americans for the return voyage home enables students to view the historical development of our nation in terms of Columbus' calculated and uncalculated risks, and the Native Americans' subsequent oppression. Similarly,

110

knowing that there are different ways to compute with and conceptualize *Pi*, and that the search for *Pi*'s precise value has influenced modern research relating to the science of chaos, enables students to form important questions that may lead to deeper understanding of geometry and mathematical functions. Fostering appreciation for a multiplicity of truths and options is the "real" mission of education because "real" problems are rarely unidimensional.

In one 3rd grade classroom, a teacher formed "consultant groups." Each student became a consultant on a self-selected topic and was responsible for keeping the rest of the class informed about that topic. Each consultant belonged to a small group of students who were charged with questioning each other in order to learn about the chosen topics.

One student became quite knowledgeable about volcanoes—so much so, in fact, that he gave "lectures" on the topic to other classes. One day, the student was describing to his group how volcanoes develop in certain regions. As his group members considered this new information, one student asked him about whether a volcano could be developing underneath the school. If it were possible, he wanted to know how they would know if one were developing. The student-consultant carefully pondered this question and said, "I don't think that volcanoes could develop here, but I'm not sure. But, I think we would know if a volcano were developing here."

"How?" one of the other students asked.

"Well," the student-consultant responded, "if a volcano were under the school, the grass would be turning brown from the heat. As long as the grass is green, I think we're safe."

Discourse with one's peer group is a critical factor in learning and development. Schools need to create settings that foster such interaction.

8. Constructivist teachers seek elaboration of students' initial responses.

Initial responses are just that—*initial* responses. Students' first thoughts about issues are not necessarily their final thoughts nor their best thoughts. Through elaboration, students often reconceptualize and assess their own errors. For example, one middle school mathematics teacher assigned his class problems in a textbook. A student, looking quite confused, asked the teacher if her approach to solving one of the problems was appropriate. The teacher asked the student to explain what she had done. As she was explaining her approach in a step-by-step manner, she recognized her own procedural error. She smiled and said, "I forgot to multiply *both* sides of the equation by "x." The teacher based his responses to the student on the premise that he could learn more about what teaching steps to take in subsequent lessons with the student than he could learn from simply fixing the mistake for her.

Occasionally, perhaps often, the adult filter through which teachers hear student responses fails to capture the students' meanings. Student elaboration enables adults to understand more clearly how students do and do not think about a concept. For example, a colleague of ours was having a discussion with his five-year-old daughter about the relative merits of living in the suburbs versus New York City. Their family had visited New York several times, and the young girl was curious about who lived there. After a few minutes, she mentioned that 42nd Street was in New York. Her father agreed, and asked her if she could name other streets in New York. She mentioned 52nd Street and 62nd Street. Her father asked her what street was above 62nd Street.

"72nd Street," she replied. Then 82nd Street, 92nd Street, and 102nd Street. Her father was now convinced that his daughter was able to count by tens, and he asked her what was below 42nd Street.

"The subway," she replied.

Students and teachers often discover how disparate their perspectives sometimes are. It's only through that discovery that individuals can engage in the process of trying to reconcile the two.

9. Constructivist teachers engage students in experiences that might engender contradictions to their initial hypotheses and then encourage discussion.

Cognitive growth occurs when an individual revisits and reformulates a current perspective. Therefore, constructivist teachers engage students in experiences that might engender contradictions to students' current hypotheses. They then encourage discussions of hypotheses and perspectives. Contradictions are constructed by learners. Teachers cannot know what will be perceived as a contradiction by students; this is an internal process.

But teachers can and must challenge students' present conceptions, knowing that the challenge only exists if the students *perceive* a contradiction. Teachers must, therefore, use information about the students' present conceptions, or points of view, to help them understand which notions students may accept or reject as contradictory.

Students of all ages develop and refine ideas about phenomena and then tenaciously hold onto these ideas as eternal truths. Even in the face of "authoritative" intervention and "hard" data that challenge their views, students typically adhere staunchly to their original notions. Through experiences that might engender contradictions, the frameworks for these notions weaken, causing students to rethink their perspectives and form new understandings. Consider the following example:

During an 11th grade discussion about the causes of World War I, one student contended with great conviction that the assassination of the Archduke Ferdinand of Austria caused the war. The teacher then asked, "If the Archduke had not been assassinated, can you tell us what would have happened with the economy and politics of the region?"

After a moment's thought, the student said, "I guess they wouldn't have changed that much."

The teacher then asked, "Would anything else have changed? How about Germany's quest to rule Europe?"

The student replied, "I can't think of anything that would have changed, except that maybe the Archduke would still be alive."

"Then," continued the teacher, "what was it that made this event the cause of the war?"

The student, now quite enmeshed in thought, said, "I guess that maybe it [the war] could have happened anyway. But, the killing of Austria's Archduke gave the Germans an excuse to begin their plan to conquer all of Europe. When Russia and France jumped in to help Serbia, the Germans declared war on them, too. But, I think I see what you mean. It was probably going to happen anyway. It just happened sooner."

Note that this elaborate explanation didn't come from the teacher. It came from the student. Note also that the student said, "I think I see what you mean," as if the meaning came from the teacher. But it did not. The meaning was constructed by the student

113

who was ready and able to understand a different point of view. When the student revealed his original perspective, the teacher was presented with the opportunity to intervene; but the contradiction was constructed by the student.

In this example, the teacher challenged the student's thinking with questions. The questions provided a mechanism for the student to reveal very sophisticated understandings of the events and political subcurrents. The teacher never directly told the student to look at the assassination as a catalyst rather than a cause. She simply wanted to present a way for the student to consider this perspective as an option. The student quickly embraced this view. Some other students in the class didn't distinguish between a catalytic event and a causal event. They didn't construct the same "contradiction" that this student constructed. The teacher then directed the class discussion to other students with subsequent questions such as: "Who also thinks that war would have just happened sooner?" "Why?" "Who disagrees?" "For what reason?" Without acknowledging one answer as better than another, everyone can participate and listen to others.

10. Constructivist teachers allow wait time after posing questions.

Several years ago, as part of its professional development efforts, a school district hired a graduate student to tapescript lessons in individual classrooms. The project was organized to provide feedback to teachers about their instructional practices: several one-minute snippets were tape recorded during a lesson, and then transcribed into writing for the teachers' reflection. One teacher, generally acknowledged to be highly skilled, was appalled to discover that she asked and answered questions in virtually the same breath. Students had no time to think about the questions she asked and quickly learned simply to wait for her to answer her own questions.

Similarly, another teacher found out that she had inadvertently orchestrated competition in her classroom. The first two or three students to raise their hands were, by and large, the only ones ever called on. If students didn't get their hands in the air immediately, they were effectively locked out of the "discussion."

These two examples illustrate the importance of wait time. In every classroom, there are students who, for a variety of reasons, are not prepared to respond to questions or other stimuli immediately. They process the world in different ways. Classroom environments that require immediate responses prevent these students from thinking through issues and concepts thoroughly, forcing them, in effect, to become spectators as their quicker peers react. They learn over time that there's no point in mentally engaging in teacher-posed questions because the questions will have been answered before they have had the opportunity to develop hypotheses.

Another reason students need wait time is that, as we have discussed, the questions posed by teachers are not always the questions heard by the students. The Gatling gun approach to asking and answering questions does not provide an opportunity for the teacher to sense the manner in which most of the students have understood the questions. Besides increasing wait time after questioning in large-group formats, we have had success with posing questions and then encouraging small groups of students to consider them before the whole group is invited back together to report on the deliberations. This format allows the teacher to call on students to deliver the group's initial responses without putting anyone on the spot. In addition, any student in the group can submit a "minority report." Thus, teachers take sensitive leadership over the orchestration of classroom dialogue and provide opportunities for all students to participate in different ways while encouraging students' intellectual autonomy with regard to concept formation.

11. Constructivist teachers provide time for students to construct relationships and create metaphors.

In one 2nd grade classroom, students were given magnets to explore. In a short time, almost all of the students had discovered that one end of a magnet attracted the other magnet while the opposite end repelled it. Soon, most of the students discovered that if one of the magnets were turned around, the magnets that had attracted each other now repelled each other. This activity took nearly 45 minutes, during which some students went beyond these initial relationships and joined forces with their peers to create magnetic "trains," and to create patterns with iron filings. A great number of relationships, patterns, and theories were generated during this activity, and none of them came from the teacher. The teacher structured and mediated the activity and provided the necessary time and material for learning to occur, but the students constructed the relationships themselves.

Encouraging the use of metaphor is another important way to facilitate learning. People of all ages use metaphors to bolster their understandings of concepts. One kindergarten student, after a field trip to pick strawberries at a local farm, ran home to his parents saying "You should have been there. It was a red heaven."

At an inservice seminar offered to experienced teachers and administrators on the topic of educational change, participants were asked to think of metaphors for the process of change in their work settings. One participant likened change to the making of wine: The seeds must be planted in fertile ground; the grapes must be harvested at the right moment; and the wine then must be aged in vats or bottles. Another participant thought of educational change as a symphony orchestra: There must be a conductor who decides what pieces shall be played and who helps all the musicians to play together. A third participant saw change as akin to preparing a meal: There is a chef who selects the menu, chooses complementary condiments, applies them according to a recipe (or whim), and lets the food cook until it is ready for consumption. Metaphors help people to understand complex issues in a holistic way and to tinker mentally with the parts of the whole to determine whether the metaphor works. And all of this takes time.

12. Constructivist teachers nurture students' natural curiosity through frequent use of the learning cycle model.

The learning cycle model has a long history in science education. The most popular description of this model was published by Atkin and Karplus (1962). Highlighting the important role of self-regulation in the learning process, the model describes curriculum development and instruction as a three-step cycle.

First, the teacher provides an open-ended opportunity for students to interact with purposefully selected materials. The primary goal of this initial lesson is for students to generate questions and hypotheses from working with the materials. This step has historically been called "discovery." Next, the teacher provides the "concept introduction" lessons aimed at focusing the students' questions, providing related new vocabulary, framing with students their proposed laboratory experiences, and so forth. The third step, "concept application," completes the cycle after one or more iterations of the discovery-concept introduction sequence. During concept application, students work on new problems with the potential for evoking a fresh look at the concepts previously studied.

Note that this cycle stands in contrast to the ways in which most curriculum, syllabi, and published materials present learning, and the ways in which most teachers were taught to teach. In the traditional model, concept introduction comes first, followed by concept application activities. Discovery, when it occurs, usually takes place after introduction and application, and with only the "quicker" students who are able to finish their application tasks before the rest of the class.

Let's take a look at how this cycle evolved in a 9th grade earth science classroom. In this classroom, the teacher told the students about the Chinook winds, the warm, dry, fast winds that blow down from the Rocky Mountains into the region just east of the mountains. The winds can be 40°-50° warmer than the surrounding air. In this example, the material made available for discovery purposes was a scenario for the students to consider. The teacher asked the students to work in small groups to generate a diagram that could explain why this occurrence might happen. As the groups began to work, the teacher listened to his students' deliberations, intervening in different ways dependent on the course of the dialogue occurring among the students. He asked a group that was "stuck" to begin by drawing the vegetation on the sides of the mountain. While trying to do the drawing, the students began to talk about rainfall, where it comes from, the patterns of cloud movement, and so on. At that point, the teacher moved to a group of students having a conversation about how hot air rises. The teacher asked another group, "Why does the warm wind move down if hot air rises?"

One girl in the group said emphatically, "That's what I don't understand?" Music to a constructivist teacher's ears!

117

The teacher said: "You know what your problem is now. Don't forget that the wind is fast, too." And the teacher moved on to students with whom he had not yet interacted that day.

What was the concept introduction to follow this discovery opportunity? The teacher wanted to introduce the concept of adiabatic pressure—a most sophisticated concept that without consideration of heat gain and heat loss, wind speed, and moisture conditions is largely inaccessible. The Chinook winds activity allowed the teacher to assess what elements of the concept are within the students' intellectual reach.

* * *

These 12 descriptors highlight teacher practices that help students search for their own understandings rather than follow other people's logic. The descriptors can serve as guides that may help other educators forge personal interpretations of what it means to become a constructivist teacher.

References

Atkin, J.M., and R. Karplus. (1962). "Discovery or Invention?" *Science Teacher.* 29, 5: 45.

Cooper, L., D. Johnson, R. Johnson, and F. Welderson. (1980). "The Effects of Cooperative, Competitive, and Individualistic Experiences in Inter-Personal Attractions Among Heterogeneous Peers." *The Journal of Social Psychology* 111: 243-252.

Johnson, D., and R. Johnson. (1981). "Effects of Cooperative and Indi-vidualistic Learning Experiences on Interethnic Interaction." *Journal of Educational Psychology* 73, 3, 444-449.

Slavin, R. (1990). *Cooperative Learning Theory, Research and Practice.* Englewood Cliffs, N.J.: Prentice-Hall.

10

Pursuing Meaningful Victories

Be ashamed to die until you have won some victory for humanity.

Horace Mann

Five 7th grade students were working with the librarian after their social studies class reacted to the U.S. Constitution's "three-fifths rule," which stipulated that five votes by African-American males counted as three votes by white males. One of the five students seemed rather impatient and pre-occupied. The following dialogue ensued:

Librarian: Ava, you seem far away. Is anything wrong?

Ava: Why do we have to spend so much time talking about this?

Librarian: We're talking about it so that you'll understand it better. I want you to learn about it.

Ava: We don't have time to learn it. We have to get the assignment done. Mr. Smith is going to collect it.

Schools throughout America are filled with students like Ava, students who have been acculturated to devalue thinking, to feel uneasy about in-depth analysis, and to view anything other than rapid coverage of the curriculum as wasting time. These students are frequently successful in school. They study, complete their assignments, pass their tests, and receive good grades. Yet, these are not meaningful victories. They are the victories of form over substance, of superficiality over engagement, of coverage over depth.

Every day, millions of students enter school wanting to learn, hoping to be stimulated, engaged, and treated well, and hoping to find meaning in what they do. And every day that we, as educators, stimulate and challenge our students to focus their minds on meaningful tasks, to think about important issues, and to construct new understandings of their worlds, we—and they—achieve a meaningful victory.

Bold Actions and Changes

Meaningful victories require bold actions. Many recent school reform initiatives are built on the time-honored but terribly flawed test-teach-test model of instruction. The call for national standards and national examinations and the call for more stringent exit outcomes at all levels are structured around this model. Ironically, these initiatives are yoked to the very approaches that have brought about the need for school reform in the first place. They are attempts to standardize goals and develop assessment devices. They are journeys down the same old roads, and are, therefore, familiar, timid, and superficial as reform initiatives. The core of the matter is still not being addressed.

Assessment and standards are undeniably important issues, but they have always been and remain the tail that wags the dog. Meaningful school reform must address the central unit of the entire enterprise, the classroom, and must seek to alter the ways teaching and learning have traditionally been thought to interact in that unit.

Creating constructivist classrooms requires bold changes—institutional adaptations that break significantly from past and current practices to create new structures and norms for the institutions undergoing change. We have six suggestions.

1. Structure preservice and inservice teacher education around constructivist principles and practices.

Educators need information regarding developmental principles and strategies for enabling students to construct their own understandings of important concepts. So much of what aspiring and practicing teachers are taught is rooted in the behavioral soil of stimulus/response theory. But this soil has been used for too many years, and is becoming more widely seen as nutrient-deficient. It's time to replant our ideas about teaching and learning in richer fields.

Rather than presenting Skinner and Thorndike in the educational psychology course required of undergraduates, expose students to the research of Piaget, Vygotsky, Elkind, Dewey, and Gardner. Rather than teaching undergraduates about mastery learning and the Hunter Model in their methods courses, expose them to the important methodological work of Sigel, Fosnot, Forman, Wadsworth, Labinowicz, Duckworth, Karplus, and Joyce and Weil.

The philosophical underpinnings of the theories and practices to which preservice teachers are exposed have a lasting impact on their perception of the teaching role. Once practicing, teachers have an even richer context in which to develop and apply their newly emerging theories and methodologies. Both preservice and inservice teacher education must promote teaching practices that mediate student construction of their own understandings, therefore, teacher education programs must themselves be constructivist-based (Brooks 1984, Brooks and Brooks 1987, Loucks-Horsley et al. 1990, Fosnot 1989 in press).

We have found that teachers more readily understand and practice constructivist methodologies when (1) they are exposed to specific programs and approaches with constructivist frameworks, such as whole-language teaching approaches, manipulative mathematics programs, hands-on science models, cooperative learning techniques, and interactive/flexible grouping paradigms, and (2) they have classroom support for altering their practices, such as peer coaching, script-taping of lessons, and team teaching. But unless teachers are given ample opportunities to learn in constructivist settings and construct for themselves educational visions through which they can reflect on educational practices,

121

the instructional programs they learn will be trivialized into "cook-book" procedures.

2. Jettison most standardized testing and make assessment meaningful for students.

In Chapter 1, we indicate that overhauling assessment proce-dures is a promising reform proposal that, by itself, does not go far enough. In conjunction with restructured teaching practices, however, the restructuring of assessment procedures can be highly significant. (See Chapter 8 for several classroom strategies.)

By the time most students enter 3rd grade, they have taken several high-stakes, standardized tests and are already viewed as either academically successful or unsuccessful by the adults in the schools they attend. Test results become not the means to assess movement toward ends and to shift directions if necessary, but the ends themselves. Schools over-emphasize test results—teachers gauge their own efficacy by them, parents fixate on them, and students come to fear them. Ultimately, test results obscure oppor-tunities to honor and value individual differences and instead translate differences into classifications that place, even trap, students in a range of settings such as remedial and gifted pro-grams.

Further, most tests, particularly fact-based, multiple-choice tests, are unreliable as indices of what students do or do not "know." In preparing for such tests, students must guess which discrete bits of information the teacher—or the state—considers most important. Concepts are often completely lost in the whirl of activity that surrounds preparing students to take tests.

Worst of all, in most school settings, testing is not part of the instructional program. It is a separate event, apart from instruc-tion, with a life of its own. Teaching often ceases completely in preparation for testing.

In a constructivist setting, assessment of student learning is done naturally within the context of lessons and activities. Teach-ers analyze student products and exhibitions as benchmarks and garner information for use in developing future activities and informing ongoing practice.

Before moving on, two points need to be made. First, we are not calling for a national set of "authentic" tasks for all students in a particular grade. Authenticity is in the eye of the beholder, and what is authentic to the adult task developer may not be especially authentic to many students. And, what is authentic in one setting may not be authentic in another. Under such conditions, we will have simply replaced one accountability paradigm that drives instruction (testing) with another that does the same thing ("authentic" task assessment).

Second, if assessment measures learning, and learning is idiosyncratic, then it is unlikely that one task, one portfolio protocol, or one mode of exhibition could be appropriate for all students. Some students are still being denied the opportunity to demonstrate what they have learned in the most effective manner for them. This is why we reiterate the importance of student/student and teacher/student interplay in revealing what has been learned: teachers must structure the environment to recognize and accept multiple forms of exhibition, and students must select those that are appropriate for them.

3. Focus resources more on teachers' professional development than on textbooks and workbooks.

For many years, there has been growing pressure from politicians, legislators, state-level administrators, and even local school boards to make education "teacher-proof." The thinking is that because some teachers are less competent than others, the experience for students must be standardized by requiring all teachers to use the same materials and teaching methodologies. The primary problem with this line of reasoning is that the teachers who were unable to structure their own materials and methodologies in a competent fashion are the very same teachers who have difficulty implementing standardized curriculums and approaches. The students in their classes continue to suffer, as do students in all classes required to use teacher-proof materials and slavishly follow teacher-proof syllabi.

Well-educated and supported, teachers are mediators between students and the environment as students come to understand complex concepts. These teachers structure the environment and set the intellectual and social tone in the classroom. Ill-educated and unsupported, teachers merely disseminate information and distribute supplies as students move through a fixed curriculum.

The purchase of teacher-proof materials diverts resources from professional development.

School systems that view their mission as fitting the curriculum to the child generally give teachers much freedom in selecting instructional methodologies and materials. School systems that view their mission as fitting the child to the curriculum generally hold the curriculum as sacrosanct and require uniformity of materials and methodologies. It's our view that the professional development of teachers ultimately has a far greater impact on student learning than do standardized curriculums.

The term professional development refers not only to inservice education but to the formation of focused teacher support groups, the scheduling of common planning time, conference attendance, the use of external and in-house consultants, and sustained peer coaching. All of these activities need to be bound together by a common thread, or vision, relating to the education of students.

4. Eliminate letter and number grades.

Just as testing drives instruction, grading drives testing. We have asked many teachers why they give fact-based multiple-choice tests to their students. Most teachers, particularly secondary school teachers, indicate that test results enable them to give "objective" grades to their students. Many secondary teachers also report that they feel compelled to give grades because colleges and universities want to be able to differentiate among students who apply for admission.

Our concern has to do with the invidious effects of grading, both overt and subtle. Overtly, grades communicate that some students are "smarter" than others. Grades are used to place students into tracks, which usually have a profound effect on students' options for college, career, and income. Subtly, grades become the rewards and punishments for school performance. The pursuit of the rewards and avoidance of the punishments overwhelm the search for understanding. For example, several elementary school reading programs across the nation reward students with trinkets, pizzas, or stickers for the number of books read: the more books, the larger the reward. The intrinsic value of reading becomes obscured in these programs by the quest for the rewards (Kohn 1986). The importance of learning and understanding is demeaned. Naturally, this has a correlative effect on classroom dynamics. Returning to the interaction between Ava and the librarian, the real message in Ava's comments was: "let's cover the material so that I can hand in my assignment and get a good grade." Students come to view the struggle to construct understanding as an impediment to the achievement of good grades.

5. Form school-based study groups focused on human developmental principles.

An understanding of human development is very important. Most educators have learned about curriculum and instructional methodologies by designing and creating their own. Few educators, however, have learned much about development through their own research and design. Most information about development has been "handed down" in large lecture classes taken to earn the necessary credits for teacher certification.

To create schools that recognize, value, and respond to the cognitive, social, and emotional needs of students, educators need to carefully study those factors in the context of their own settings on an ongoing basis. Schools *are* research institutions. Schools have access to important data on student development all day long. We need to start systematically collecting, analyzing, and using these data to inform classroom practices.

Study groups comprised of interested core participants need to take on leadership roles in defining that which they want to study. It might be a policy that doesn't seem to work, a student who isn't making it, a concept that no one learns, or myriad other issues. Together, the members of the study group guide each other in formulating a better understanding of how they can make their school, in the particular domain under study, a more humane, growth producing setting. We have found that as the study group matures, so does its outreach to other parts of the school.

6. Require annual seminars on teaching and learning for administrators and school board members.

Administrators directly supervise and evaluate teachers, and boards of education set the educational "missions" for their districts. Teachers interested in teaching for understanding will be

125

placed in great conflict if their administrators write lesson observations and end-of-the-year evaluations that suggest a more traditional approach and if their boards of education view standardized
test scores as the primary indicators of student learning.

Several years ago, a building principal observed a fairly traditional 2nd grade lesson on spelling. Students were asked to place
each of the 15 words from their spelling lists into sentences. This
was supposed to demonstrate both the students' ability to spell the
words and their understanding of each word's meaning. Many
students appeared disinterested.

In the post-observation conference, the principal and teacher
focused on student behaviors and products and together explored
options for engaging students in writing groups and word study
groups. They settled upon introducing spelling through writing.
Administrators and teachers able to engage in such discussions
can favorably affect the type of educational program offered to
students. One way to foster this is through the establishment of
annual seminars that address pedagogical issues for administrators and board of education members. These seminars help teachers, administrators, and board of education members "speak the
same language" and focus on students.

New Images

Bold changes require the establishment of new norms and
structures for schools and school systems. This is no easy task. But
the alternative is the status quo or new versions of it.

What images are evoked in most people's minds upon hearing
the word "school"? Raising one's hand before answering questions,
listening to teachers and taking notes, taking tests, lugging textbooks from class to class, writing book reports, standing in straight
lines, seeking permission to visit the restroom. These are the very
images, practices, and expectations upon which schooling has
been structured since the first common schools were erected well
over a century ago. They are images of control, not learning.

A new set of images, reflective of new practices, is needed—
images that portray the student as a thinker, a creator, and a
constructor. Schools can become settings in which students are

encouraged to develop hypotheses, to test out their own and others' ideas, to make connections among "content" areas, to explore issues and problems of personal relevance (either existing or emerging), to work cooperatively with peers and adults in the pursuit of understanding, and to form the disposition to be life-long learners. The old images of school do not speak directly to the central issue of school reform—ways to evoke student learning through their search for understanding. The images of constructivism do.

References

Brooks, M. (1984). "A Constructivist Approach to Staff Development." *Educational Leadership* 42, 3: 23-27.

Brooks, M.G., and J.G. Brooks. (Fall 1987). "Becoming a Teacher for Thinking: Constructivism, Change, and Consequence." *The Journal of Staff Development* 8, 3: 16-20.

Cremin, L.A., ed. (1957). *The Republic and the School: Horace Mann on the Education of Free Men.* New York: Teachers College Press.

Fosnot, C.T., (in press). "Rethinking Science Education: A Defense of Piagetian Constructivism." *Journal for Research in Science Education.*

Fosnot, C.T. (1989). *Enquiring Teachers, Enquiring Learning: A Constructivist Approach for Teaching.* New York: Teachers College Press.

Joyce, B., and M. Weil. (1972). *Models of Teaching.* New York: Prentice-Hall.

Kohn, A. (1986). *No Contest: The Case Against Competition.* Boston, Houghton-Mifflin.

Loucks-Horsley, S., J.G. Brooks, M.O. Carlson, P. Kuerbis, D. Marsh, M. Padilla, H. Pratt, and K. Smith. (1990). *Developing and Supporting Teachers for Science Education in the Middle Years.* Andover, Mass.: The National Center for Improving Science Education.

Bibliography

Arlin, P.K. (1985). "Teaching Thinking: A Developmental Perspective." *IMPACT on Instructional Improvement* 19,3.

Athey, I.J., and D.O. Rubadeau, eds. (1970). *Educational Implications of Piaget's Theory*. Waltham, Mass.: Ginn & Co.

Atkin, J.M., and R. Karplus. (1962). "Discovery or Invention?" *Science Teacher* 29, 5: 45.

Bamberger, J., E. Duckworth, and M. Lampert. (1981). "An Experiment in Teacher Development." Unpublished Manuscript. Final Report for NIE Grant # G-78-0219, Washington D.C.: National Institute of Education.

Baratta-Lorton, M. (1976). *Mathematics Their Way*. Menlo Park, Calif.: Addison-Wesley.

Beilin, H. (1965). "Learning and Operational Convergence in Logical Thought Development." *Journal of Experimental Child Psychology* 2: 317-339.

Berman, P., and M.W. McLaughlin. (1974). *A Model of Educational Change: Federal Programs Supporting Educational Change, Volume I*. Santa Monica, Calif.: Rand Corporation.

Bettelheim, B. (1966). *The Empty Fortress*. New York: Macmillan.

Bobbitt, F. (1918). *The Curriculum*. Boston: Houghton-Mifflin, Co.

Brainerd, C.J. (1978). "The Stage Question in Cognitive-Developmental Theory." *The Behavioral and Brain Sciences* 2: 173-213.

Brearley, M., ed. (1969). *The Teaching of Young Children, Some Applications of Piaget's Learning Theories*. New York: Schocken Books.

Brooks, M., and J.G. Brooks, eds. (1985). "Teaching for Thinking." *IMPACT on Instructional Improvement* 19, 3.

Brooks, M., and J.G. Brooks, eds. (1985). "Teaching for Thinking: II." *IMPACT on Instructional Improvement* 19, 4.

Brown, A.L. (1985). "Motivation to Learn and Understand: On Taking Charge of One's Own Learning." *Cognition and Instruction* 5, 4: 311-322.

Brown, F.K., and D.P. Butts. (1983). *Science Teaching: A Profession Speaks, NSTA Yearbook*. Washington D.C.

Bruner, J. (1985). "Models of the Learner." *Educational Researcher* 14, 6.

Bruner, J.S. (1968). *Toward a Theory of Instruction*. New York: Norton.

Bybee, R.W. (1986). "The Sisyphean Question in Science Education: What Should the Scientifically and Technologically Literate Person Know, Value and Do—As a Citizen?" *1985 NSTA Yearbook*. Washington, D.C.: NSTA.

Case, R. (1973). "Piaget's Theory of Child Development and its Implications." *Phi Delta Kappan* 55: 20-25.

Copeland, R.W. (1970). *How Children Learn Mathematics—Teaching Implications of Piaget's Research*. New York: MacMillan Co.

DeVries, R., and L. Kohlberg. (1987). *Programs of Early Education: The Constructivist View*. New York: Longman.

Dewey, J. (1974). "The Child and the Curriculum." In *John Dewey on Education*, edited by R.D. Archambault. Chicago: University of Chicago Press.

Dewey, J. (1933). *How We Think*. Revised Ed. New York: Heath.

Dewey, J. (1974). "The Child and the Curriculum." In *John Dewey on Education*, edited by R.D. Archambault. Chicago: University of Chicago Press.

Dewey, J.(1979). *Sources of Science Education*. New York: Liveright.

Driver, R. (1983). *The Pupil Scientist?* Philadelphia: Open University Press.

Duckworth, E. (August 1979). "Either We're Too Early and They Can't Learn It or We're too Late and They Know It Already: The Dilemma of 'Applying Piaget.'" *Harvard Educational Review* 49, 3.

Duckworth, E., J. Easley, D. Hawkins, and A. Henriques. (1990). *Science Education: A Minds-On Approach for the Elementary Years*. Hillsdale, N.J.: Lawrence Erlbaum Associates.

Eisner, E. (1982). *Cognition and Curriculum: A Basis for Deciding What to Teach*. New York: Longman.

Elkind, D. (1974). *Children and Adolescents: Interpretive Essays on Jean Piaget*. N.Y.: Oxford University Press.

Flannery, M.C. (1991). *Bitten by the Biology Bug: Essays from The American Biology Teacher*. Reston, Va.: National Association of Biology Teachers.

Flavell, J.H. (1963). *The Developmental Psychology of Jean Piaget*. Princeton, N.J.: D. Van Nostrand.

Forman, G., and D. Kuschner. (1977). *The Child's Construction of Knowledge: Piaget for Teaching Children*. Belmont, Calif.: Wadworth Co.

Forman, G., and P.B. Pufall, eds. (1988). *Constructivism in the Computer Age*. Hillsdale, N.J.: Lawrence Erlbaum Associates.

Forman, G.E. (1985). "Helping Children Ask Good Questions." In *The Wonder of It: Exploring How the World Works*, edited by B. Neugebauer. Exchange Press 21-25.

Forman, G. (1989). "Helping Children Ask Good Questions." In *The Wonder of It: Exploring How the World Works*, edited by B. Neugebauer. Redmond, Wash.: Exchange Press, Inc.

Forman, G. (1987). "The Constructivism Perspective." In *Approaches to Early Childhood Education*, edited by J.L. Roopnarine, and J.E. Johnson. Columbus, Ohio: Merrill Publishing Co., pp. 71-84.

Foshay, A.W. (Summer 1991). "The Curriculum Matrix: Transcendence and Mathematics." *Journal of Curriculum and Supervision* 6, 4: 277-293.

Frazier, R. (1988). "Beginning Without a Conclusion." *The Science Teacher* 55, 5.

Fuller, M. (1982). *The Meaning of Educational Change*. New York: Teachers' College Press.

Furth, H.G., and H. Wachs. (1974). *Thinking Goes to School*. New York: Oxford University Press.

Furth, H.G. (1970). *Piaget for Teachers*. Englewood Cliffs, N.J.: Prentice-Hall.

Furth, H.G. (1980). *The World of Grownups: Children's Perceptions of Society*. New York: Elsevier.

Gardner, H. (1983). *Frames of Mind*. New York: Basic Books.

Gardner, H. (October 9, 1991a). "Making Schools More Like Museums." *Education Week*, p. 40.

Ginsburg, H.P., and B.S. Allerdice. (1984). "Children's Difficulties with School Mathematics." In *Everyday Cognition: Its Development in Social Context*, edited by B. Rogoff and J. Lave. Cambridge, Mass.: Harvard University Press, pp. 194-219.

Goodlad, J. (1975). *The Dynamics of Educational Change*. New York: McGraw-Hill.

Goodman, K. (1986). *What's Whole in Whole Language?* Portsmouth, N.H.: Heinemann.

Graves, D.H. (1983). *Writing: Teachers and Children at Work*. Portsmouth, N.H.: Heinemann.

Grennon, J. (1984). "Making Sense of Student Thinking." *Educational Leadership* 42, 3: 11-18.

Groen, G. (1978). "The Theoretical Ideas of Piaget and Educational Practice." *Impact of Research on Education: Some Case Studies*. National Academy of Education.

Haroutunian-Gordon, S. (1991). *Teaching the Soul: Teaching Through Conversation in the High School*. Chicago: The University of Chicago Press.

Harris, K.R., and M. Pressley. (March/April 1991). "The Nature of Cognitive Strategy Instruction: Interactive Strategy Construction." *Exceptional Children* pp. 392-403.

Hawkins, D. (February 1965). "Messing About in Science." *Science and Children* 2, 5.

Hawkins, D. (Spring 1983). "Nature Closely Observed." *Daedalus* 112, 2: 65-89.

Hills, G.L.C. (1989). "Students' Untutored Beliefs about Natural Phenomena: Primitive Science or Common Sense?" *Science Education* 3, 2: 155-186.

Hunt, J.McV. (1961). *Intelligence and Experience*. New York: Ronald Press.

Inhelder, B., and J. Piaget. (1958). *The Growth of Logical Thinking from Childhood to Adolescence*. New York: Basic Books.

Jacob, S. (Winter 1982). "Piaget and Education: Aspects of a Theory, Part I." *The Educational Forum*.

Jalongo, M.R. (1991). *The Role of the Teacher in the 21st Century: An Insider's View*. Bloomington, Ind.: National Educational Service.

Johnson, D.W., and R.T. Johnson. (1984). *Circles of Learning: Cooperation in the Classroom*. Alexandria, Va.: ASCD.

Kamii, C., ed. (1990). *Achievement Testing in the Early Grades: The Games Grown Ups Play*. Washington, D.C.: National Association for the Education of Young Children.

Kamii, C., and B.A. Lewis. (May 1991). "Achievement Tests in Primary Mathematics: Perpetuating Lower-Order Thinking." *Arithmetic Teacher* pp. 4-9.

Kamii, C., and R. DeVries. (1980). *Group Games in Early Education: Implications of Piaget's Theory*. Washington, D.C.: NAEYC.

Kamii, C. (September 1985). "Leading Primary Education Toward Excellence: Beyond Worksheets and Drill." *Young Children* 40, 6: 3-9.

Kamii, C., M. Manning, and G. Manning, eds. (1991). *Early Literacy: A Constructivist Foundation for Whole Language*. Washington, D.C.: National Education Association.

Kamii, C., S. Jones., and L. Joseph. (April 1991). "When Kids Make Their Own Math, They Can Make Math Their Own." *Power Line* 1, 2: 1-2.

Kamii, C. (1985). *Young Children Re-Invent Arithmetic*. New York: Teachers College Press.

Kant, I. (1960). *Education*, translated and reprinted. Ann Arbor, Mich.: University of Michigan Press.

Karplus, R. (1964). "The Science Curriculum Improvement Study—Report to the Piaget Conference." *Journal of Research in Science Teaching* 2, 3.

Katz, J., and H. Mildred. (1988). *Turning Professors into Teachers: A New Approach to Faculty Development and Student Learning*. MacMillan.

Katz, L., and S. Chard. (1986). *Engaging Children's Minds: The Project Approach to Education*. Norwood, N.J.: Ablex Publishers.

Kohlberg, L., and R. Mayer. (1972). "Development as the Aim of Education." *Harvard Educational Review* 42, 4: 449-496.

Kohlberg, L. (1976). "Moral Stages and Moralization: The Cognitive-Developmental Approach." In *Moral Development and Behavior: Theory, Research and Social Issues*, edited by T. Lickona. New York: Holt, Rinehart & Winston.

131

Kohn, A. (March 1991). "Teaching Children to Care." *Phi Delta Kappan* 72, 7: 497-506.

Lambert, M., (1984). "Teaching About Thinking and Thinking About Teaching." *Journal of Curriculum Studies* 16.

Langer, J. (1964). "Implications of Piaget's Talks for Curriculum." *Journal of Research in Science Teaching* 2, 3.

Lavatelli, C. (1973). *Piaget's Theory Applied to an Early Childhood Curriculum*. Boston: American Science and Engineering.

Lawrence, F. (December 1986). "Misconceptions of Physical Science Concepts among Elementary School Teachers." *School and Science Mathematics*, 86, 8: 654-660.

Lawson, A.E., and J.W. Renner. (September 1975). "Piagetian Theory and Biology Teaching." *The American Biology Teacher* 37, 6: 336-343.

Lieberman, A., and L. Miller. (1984). *Teachers, Their World and their Work*. Alexandria, Va.: ASCD.

Loevinger, J. (1976). *Ego Development*. San Francisco: Jossey Bass.

Lombard, A.S., R.D. Konicek, and K. Schultz. (1985). "Description and Evaluation of an Inservice Model for Implementation of a Learning Cycle Approach in the Secondary Science Classroom." *Science Education* 69, 4: 491-500.

Lombard, A.S., R.D. Konicek, and K. Schultz. (July 1985). "Description and Evaluation of an Inservice Model for Implementation of a Learning Cycle Approach in the Secondary Science Classroom." *Science Education* 69, 4: 491-500.

Loucks-Horsley, S., J.G. Brooks, M.O. Carlson, P. Kuerbis, D. Marsh, M. Padilla, H. Pratt, and K. Smith. (1990). *Developing and Supporting Teachers for Science Education in the Middle Years*. Andover, Mass.: The National Center for Improving Science Education.

Lowery, L. (1974a). *Learning About Instruction: Questioning Strategies*. University of California, Berkeley.

Lowery, L. (1974b). *Learning About Learning: Classification Abilities*. University of California, Berkeley.

Lowery, L. (1974c). *Learning About Learning: Conservation Abilities*. University of California, Berkeley.

Mallon, E.J. (January 1976). "Cognitive Development and Processes: Review of the Philosophy of Jean Piaget." *The American Biology Teacher* 38, 1.

Maxwell, N. (May 1987). "Wanted: A New Way of Thinking." *New Scientist* 14: 63.

McNally, D.W. (1977). *Piaget, Education and Teaching*. Hassocks, Sussex: Harvester Press.

Melvin, M.P. (December 1985). "How Do They Learn?" *Phi Delta Kappan* 67, 4: 306-307.

Montemayor, R., and M. Eisen. (1977). "The Development of Self-Conceptions from Childhood to Adolescence." *Developmental Psychology* 13, 44: 314-319.

Murray, D.M. (1982). *Learning By Teaching: Selected Articles on Writing and Teaching*. Upper Montclair, N.J.: Boynton Cook.

Narode, R., and J. Lochhead. (1985). "What Do You Think?" *IMPACT on Instructional Improvement* 19, 3.

National Council of Teachers of Mathematics. (1989). *Executive Summary of Curriculum and Evaluation Standards for School Mathematics*. Reston, Va.: NCTM.

Noddings, N. (1982). "Why is Piaget so Hard to Apply in the Classroom?" *Journal of Curriculum Theorizing* 5, 2.

Noddings, N., and P. Shore. (1984). *Awakening the Inner Eye: Intuition in Education*. New York: Teachers College Press.

Palmer, E.L. (1970). "The Equilibration Process: Some Implications." In *Educational Implications of Piaget's Theory*, edited by Irene Athey. Waltham: Ginn-Blaisdell.

Papert, S. (1980). *Mindstorms: Children, Computers and Powerful Ideas*. New York: Basic Books.

Peel, E.A. (1971). *The Nature of Adolescent Judgment*. New York: John Wiley & Sons, Inc.

Perrone, V. (1991). *Expanding Student Assessment*. Alexandria, Va.: ASCD.

Piaget, J. (1928). *Judgment and Reasoning in the Child*. New York: Harcourt.

Piaget, J. (1930). *The Child's Conception of Physical Causality*. New York: Harcourt.

Piaget, J. (1950, reprinted 1966). *The Psychology of Intelligence*. London: Routledge and Kegan Paul.

Piaget, J. (1954). *The Construction of Reality in the Child*. New York: Basic Books.

Piaget, J. (1955). *Language and Thought of the Child*. New York: New American Library.

Piaget, J. (1964). "Development and Learning." *Journal of Research in Science Teaching* 2, 3.

Piaget, J. (1967). *The Child's Conception of the World*. Totowa, N.J.: Littlefield, Adams & Co.

Piaget, J. (1969a). *The Child's Conception of Time*. London: Routledge and Keger Paul.

Piaget, J. (1969b). *The Mechanisms of Perception*. London: Routledge and Keger Paul.

Piaget, J. (1970). *Genetic Epistemology*. New York: Columbia University Press.

Piaget, J. (1970). *Structuralism*. New York: Basic Books.

Piaget, J. (1970). *The Science of Education and the Psychology of the Child*. New York: Orion Press.

Piaget, J. (1973). *Child and Reality*. New York: Grossman.

Piaget, J. (1974). *To Understand Is To Invent: The Future of Education*. New York: Grossman.

Piaget, J. (1987). *Possibility and Necessity: The Role of Necessity in Cognitive Development*. Minn.: University of Minnesota Press.

Piaget, J., and B. Inhelder. (1967). *The Child's Conception of Space*. New York: Norton & Co.

Piaget, J., and B. Inhelder. (1969, 1971). *The Psychology of the Child*. N.Y.: Basic Books.

Pope, M.L., and T.R. Keen. (1981). *Personal Construct Psychology and Education*. London: Academic Press.

Popkewitz, T., R. Tabachnick, and G. Wehlage. (1982). *The Myth of Educational Reform: A Study of School Responses to a Program of Change*. Madison, Wisc.: University of Wisconsin Press.

Poplin, M. (1988). "Holistic Constructivist Principles of the Teaching/Learning Process: Implications for the Field of Learning Disabilities." *Journal of Learning Disabilities* 21, 7: 401-416.

Pulaski, M.A. (1971). *Understanding Piaget*. New York: Harper & Row.

Renner, J.W., D.G. Stafford, A.E. Lawson, J.W. McKinnon, E.F. Friot, and D.H. Kellogg. (1976). *Research, Teaching and Learning With the Piaget Model*. Norman, Okla.: University of Oklahoma Press.

Resnick, L. (1987). *Education and Learning to Think*. Washington, D.C.: National Academy Press.

Resnick, L. (1984). *Education and Learning to Think*. London: The Falmer Press.

Rogers, C.R. (Winter 1987). "On the Shoulders of Giants." *The Educational Forum* 51, 2.

Rowland, S. (1984). *The Inquiring Classroom: An Approach to Understanding Children's Learning*. London: Falmer Press.

Sarason, S. (1972). *The Creation of Settings and the Future Societies*. San Francisco, Calif.: Jossey Bass.

Sarason, S. (1971). *The Culture of the School and the Problem of Change*. Boston: Allyn and Bacon.

Scardamalia, M., and C. Bereiter. (1983). "Child as Coinvestigator: Helping Children Gain Insight into Their Own Mental Processes." In *Learning and Motivation in the Classroom*, edited by S.G. Paris, G.M. Olson, and H.W. Stevenson. Hillsdale, N.J.: Lawrence Erlbaum Associates.

Schifter, D., and C. Fosnot. (1992). *Reconstructing Mathematics Education: Stories of Teachers Meeting the Challenge of Reform*. New York: Teachers College Press.

Schoenfeld, A. (1988). "When Good Teaching Leads to Bad Results: The Disasters of 'Well-Taught' Mathematics Courses." *Educational Psychologist* 23, 2: 145-166.

Schon, D. (1983). *The Reflective Practitioner*. New York: Basic Books.

Schwebel, M., and J. Raph. (1973). *Piaget in the Classroom*. New York: Basic Books.

Shapiro, B.L. (1989). "What Children Bring to Light: Giving High Status to Learners' Views and Actions in Science." *Science Education* 73, 6: 711-733.

Shayer, M., D.E. Kuchemann, and H. Wylam. (1976). "The Distribution of Piagetian Stages of Thinking in British Middle and Secondary School Children." *British Journal of Educational Psychology* 46: 164-173.

Shayer, M., and P. Adey. (1981). *Towards a Science of Science Teaching*. London: Heinemann Educational Books.

Sigel, O.E., and F.H. Hooper. (1968). *Logical Thinking in Children*. New York: Holt, Rinehart and Winston.

Sizer, T. (1984). *Horace's Compromise: The Dilemma of the American High School*. Boston: Houghton-Mifflin.

Slavin, R.E. (1990). *Cooperative Learning Theory, Research and Practice*. Englewood Cliffs, N.J.: Prentice-Hall.

Smock, C.D. (1981). *"Constructivism and Educational Practices." In New Directions in Piagetian Theory and Practice*, edited by I.E. Sigel, D.M. Brodzinsky, and R.M. Golinkoff. Hillsdale, N.J.: Lawrence Erlbaum Associates.

Thorndike, R., and E.F. Hagen. (1977). *Measurement and Evaluation in Psychology and Education*, 4th Edition. N.Y.: John Wiley and Sons.

von Glasersfeld, E. (1981). "The Concepts of Adaptation and Viability in a Radical Constructivist Theory of Knowledge." In *New Directions in Piagetian Theory and Practice*, edited by Sigel, Brodzinsky, and Golinkoff.

Vygotsky, L. (1962). *Thought and Language*. Cambridge, Mass.: MIT Press.

Weber, L., and H. Dyasi. (1985). "Language Development and Observation of the Local Environment: First Steps in Providing Primary-School Science Education for Non-Dominant Groups." *Prospects* XV, 4.

Wertsch, J. (1985). "The Concept of Internalization in Vygotsky's Account of the Genesis of Higher Mental Function." In *Culture, Communication and Cognition*, edited by J. Wertsch. Cambridge: Cambridge University Press, pp. 162-182.

Willoughby, S. (1970). *Mathematics Education for a Changing World*. Alexandria, Va.: ASCD.

Zumwalt, K. (1982). "Research on Teaching: Policy Implications for Teacher Education." In *Policy Making in Education: Eighty-First Yearbook of the National Society for the Study of Education, Part I*, edited by A. Lieberman and M. McLaughlin. Chicago: University of Chicago Press.

Zumwalt, K. (1987). "Tomorrow's Teachers: Tomorrow's Work." *Teachers College Record* 88, 3.